STUDENT'S BOOK OF ROUNDS
VIOLA EDITION

MB98162

BY MARILYN WORTH

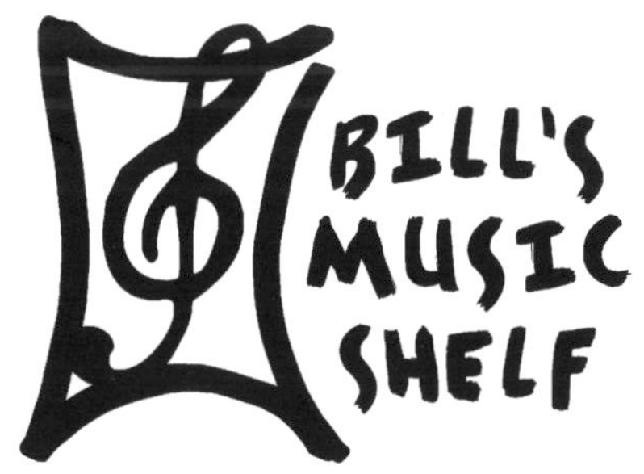

Visit us on the Web at www.melbay.com or www.billsmusicshelf.com

Table of Contents - Viola

FRESHMAN LEVEL REPERTOIRE

Adrian's Song 6

Edward's Song 7

Scotland's Burning 8

Clocks 9

Rowboat 10

Sons of the Sea 11

Come Again, Ho 12

Nearly Done 13

Alleluia, Amen 14

Dear Friend 15

Viennese Musical Clock 16

Shaker Life 17

Vesper Round 18

SOPHOMORE LEVEL REPERTOIRE

Come Again, Ho 22

Oh, Music, Sweet Music 23

Hey Nonny No 24

Peace and Prosperity 25

Good Hostess, Fill the Pot for Me 26

Invisible Fox 27

The Jolly Hunter 28

Si Cantemo 29

The Singing School 30

Shalom Chaverim 31

The Mighty Tom 32

Echo Yodel Canon 33

Orchestra 34

Reveille 35

Merry Heart 36

Dona Nobis Pacem 37

Round in G Major 38

JUNIOR LEVEL REPERTOIRE

Rose 42

Just Teasing 43

Heigh, Ho, Anybody Home? 44

Let Us Sing Together 45

Sleep, Baby, Sleep 46

The Oriole Canon 47

Who'll Buy My Roses 48

Fair Ursley 49

The Hunters 50

Sumer is Icumen In 51

Table of Contents (Continued)

All Who Sing 52
Life Span 53
The Street Cries of Oxford Town 54
The Oak 55
The Sweet Pleasures of Spring 56
Beethoven's Round 57

SENIOR LEVEL REPERTOIRE

Barcarolle 60
Pratty Naun, a Scottish Catch 61
Sing and Be Merry 62
Sing We This Roundelay 63
Ave Maria 64
Bononcini's Spring 65
Gabrial John 66
Callcott's Round 67
Now We Are Met 68
Come Hither 69
This Hour, My Bonny Lads 70
One, Two, Three 71
Tread Soft My Friend 72
Retreat 73
To the Colors 74
Haida, Haida 75
As We Mingle Our Voices, We Mingle Our Souls 76
Pachelbel's Canon 77

FRESHMAN LEVEL
REPERTOIRE

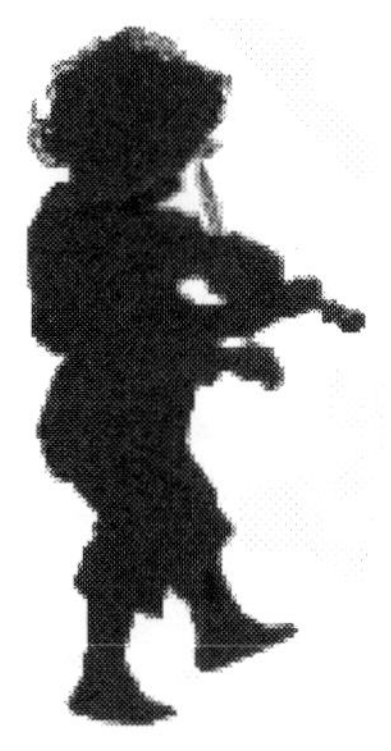

VIOLA FINGERING CHART

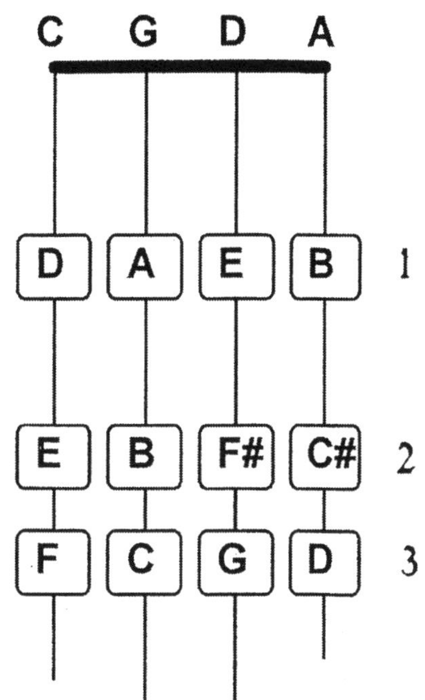

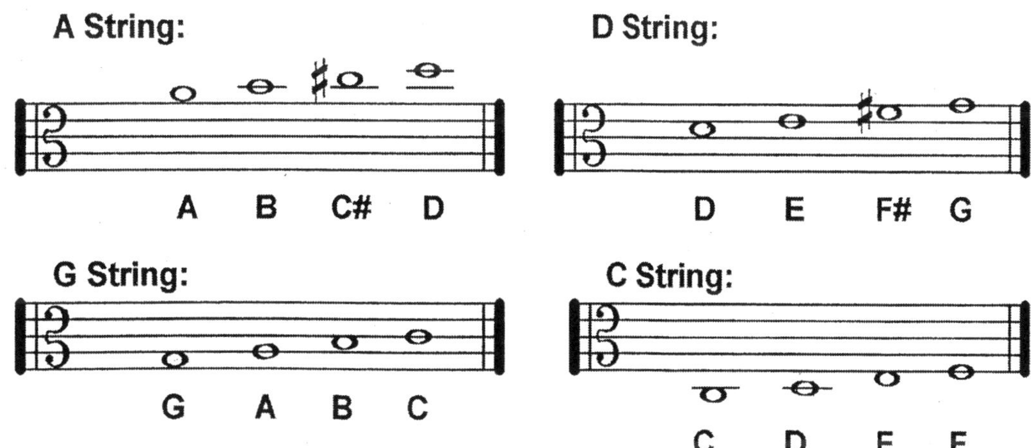

Adrian's Song

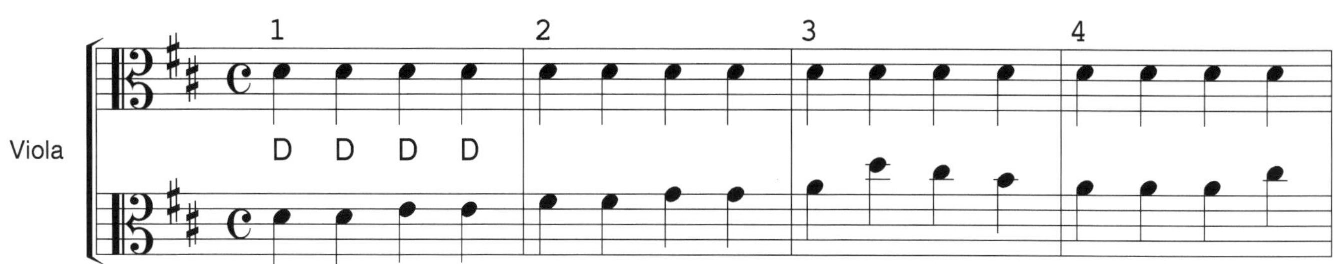

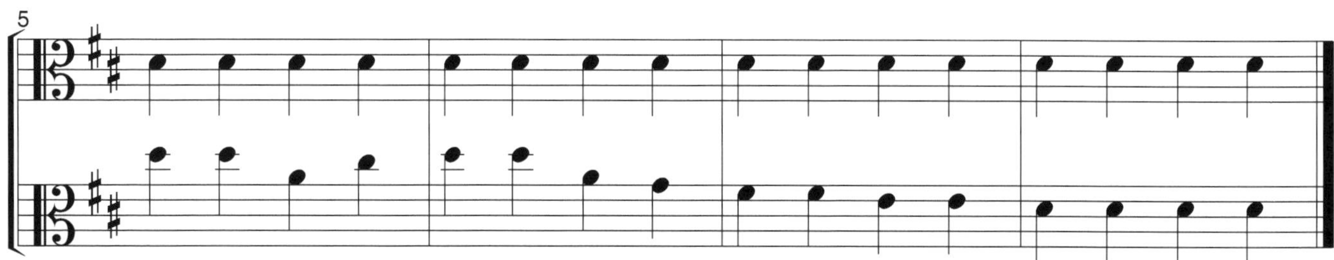

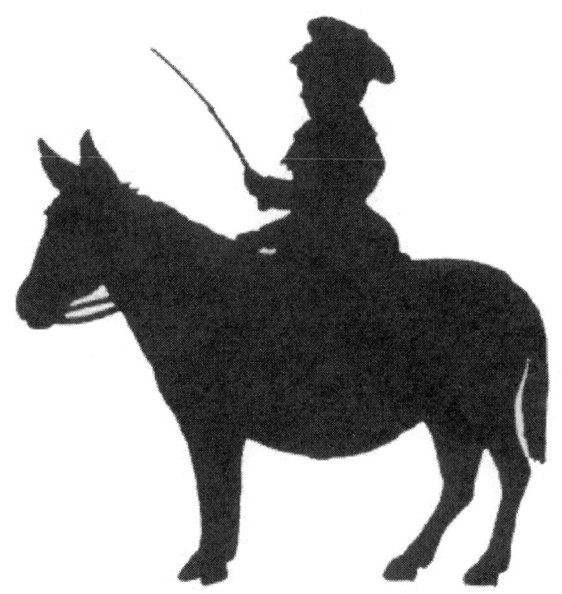

Edward's Song

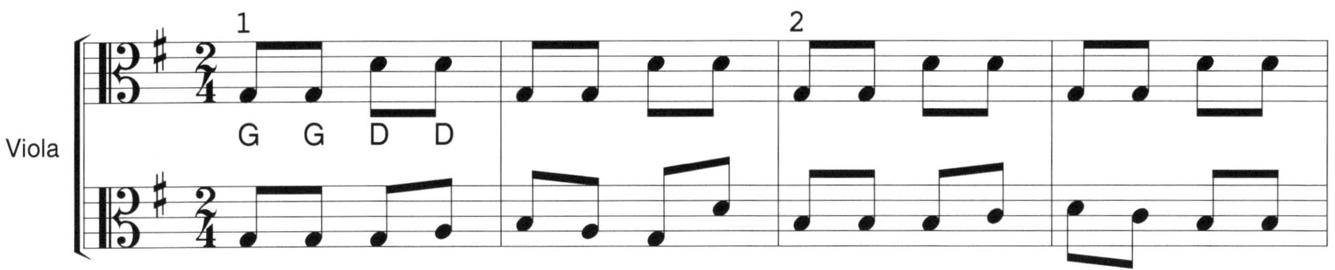

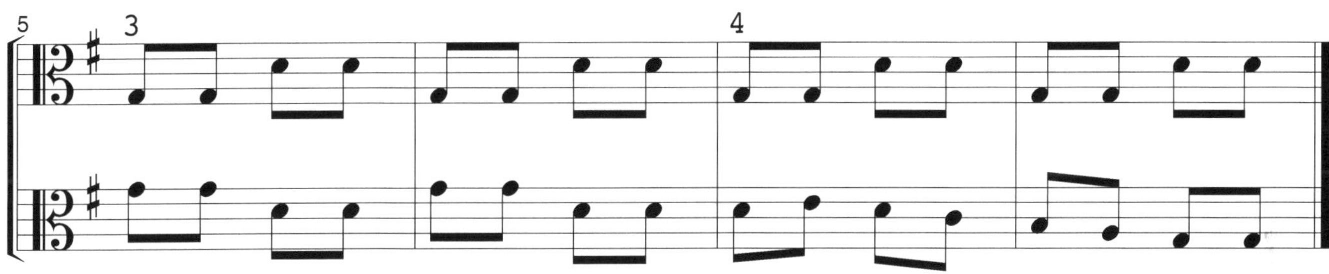

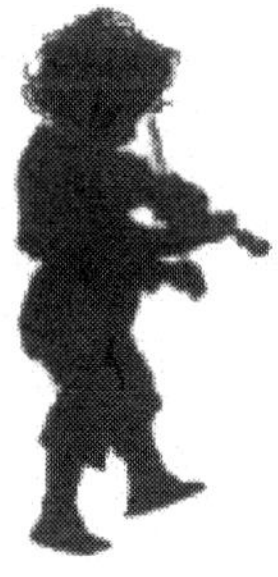

Scotland's Burning

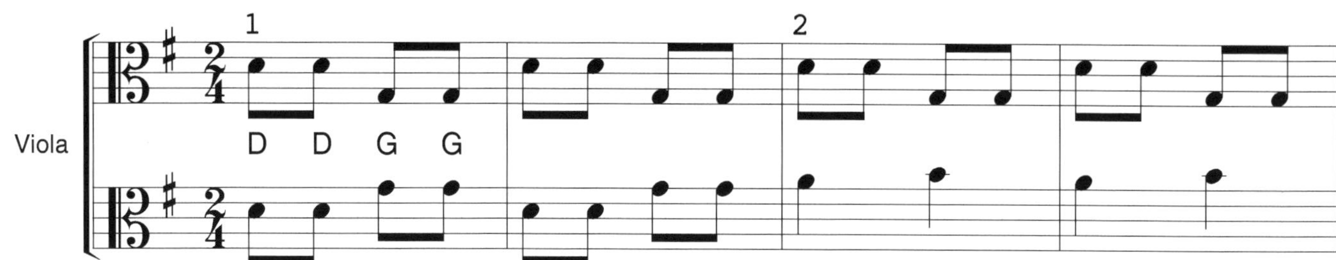

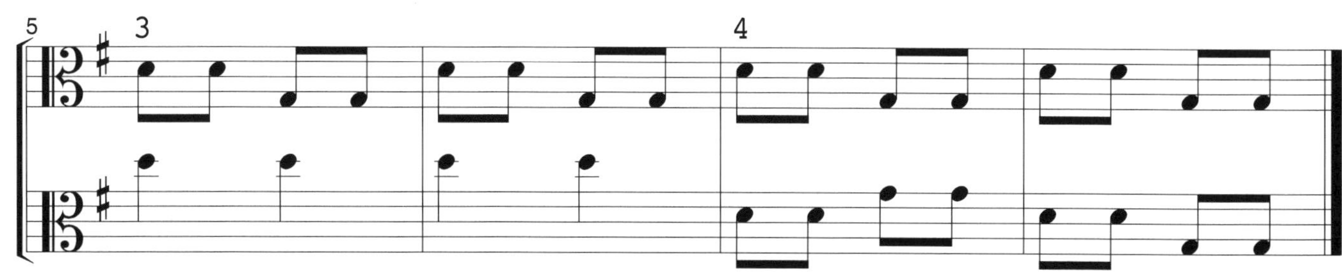

Clocks

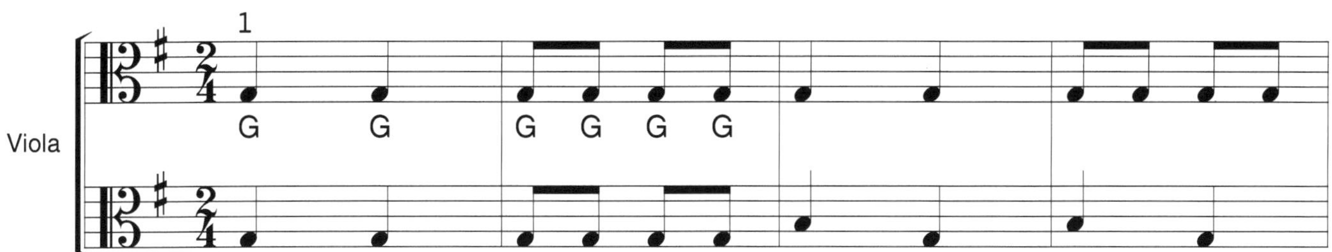

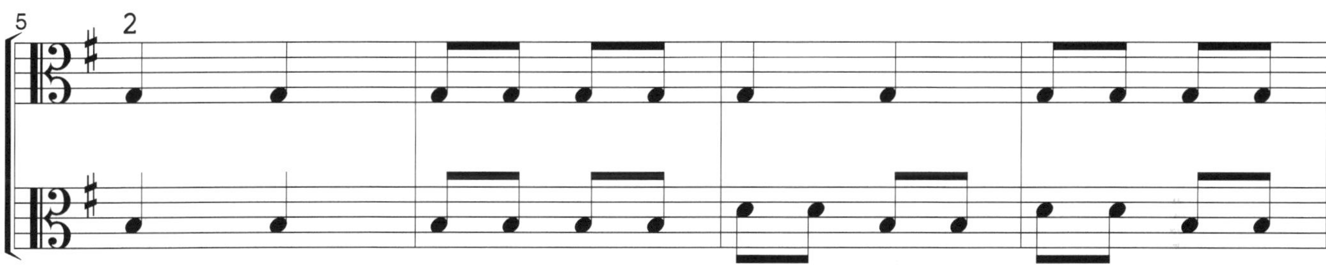

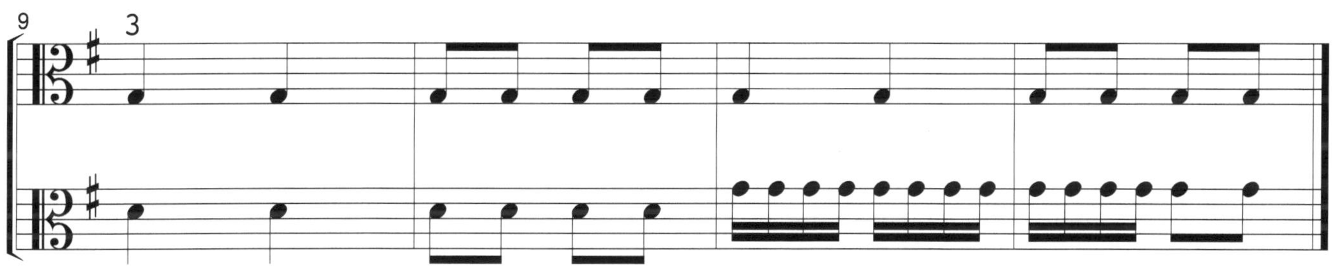

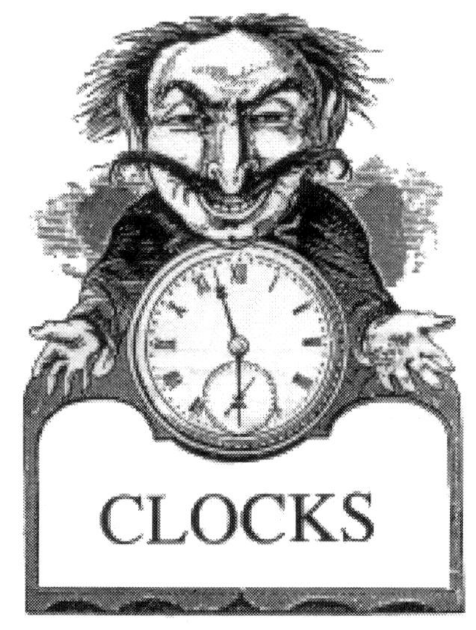

Rowboat

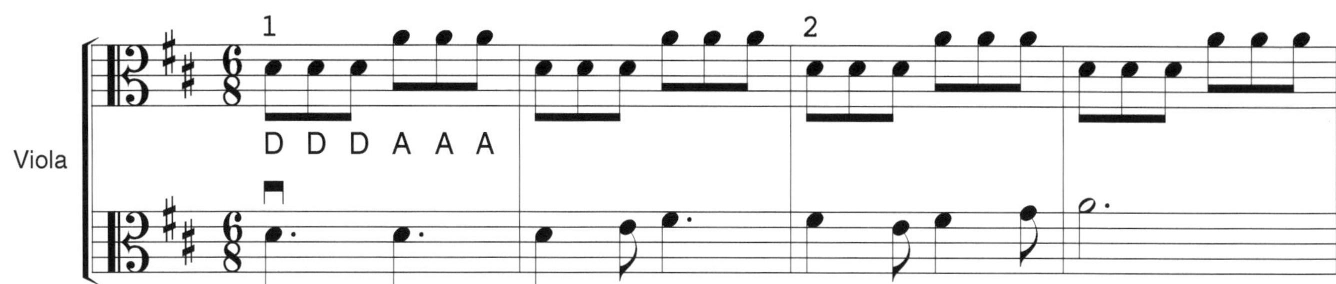

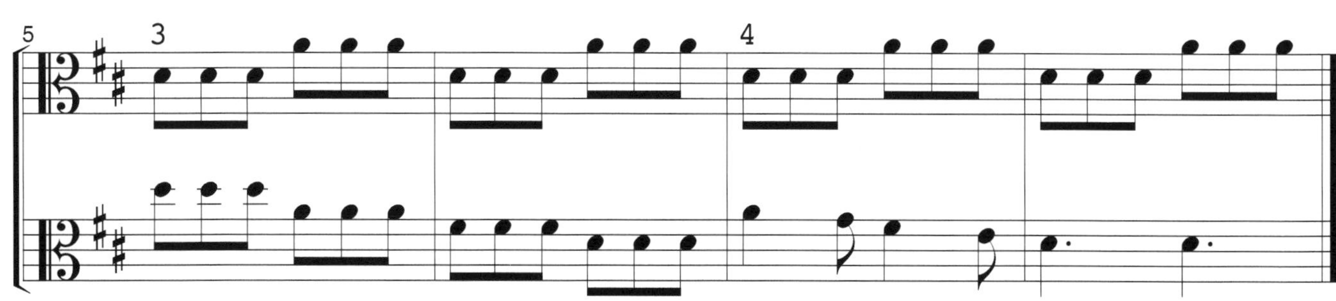

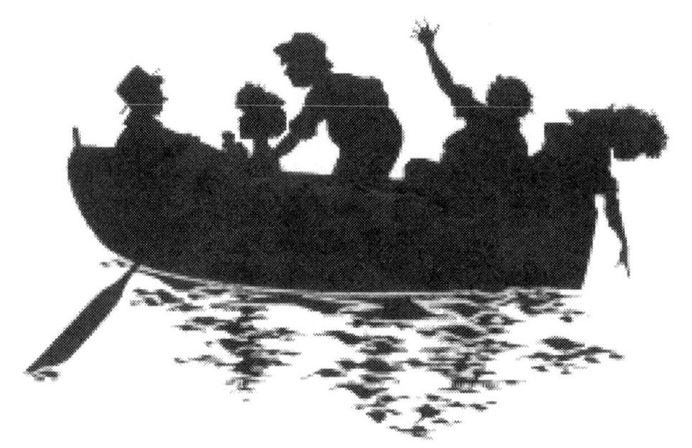

Sons of the Sea

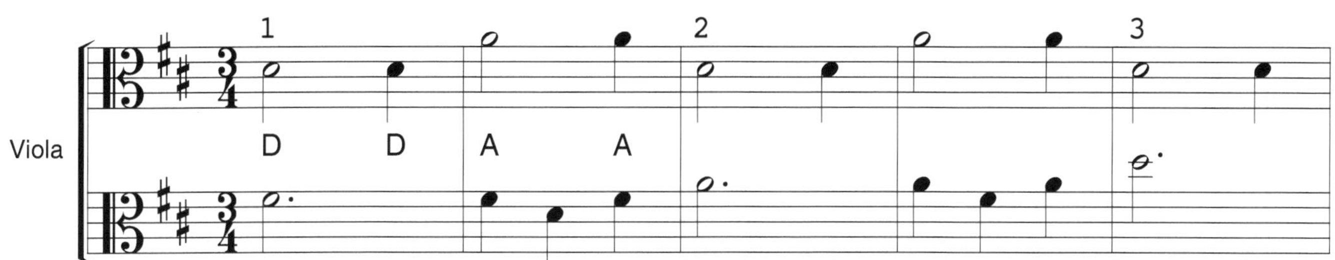

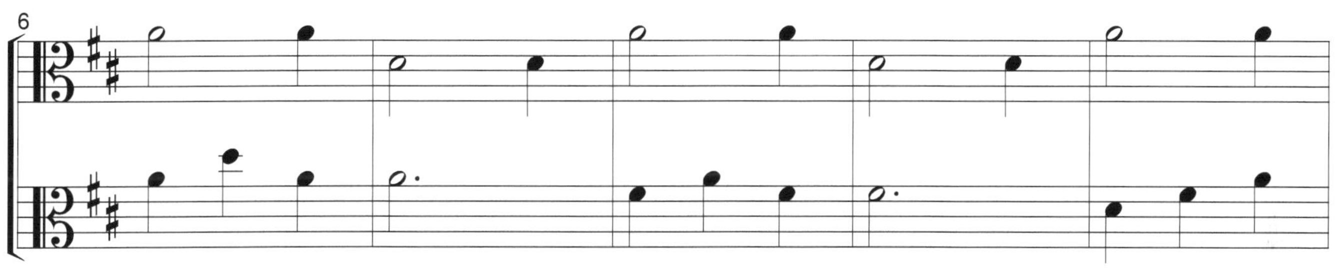

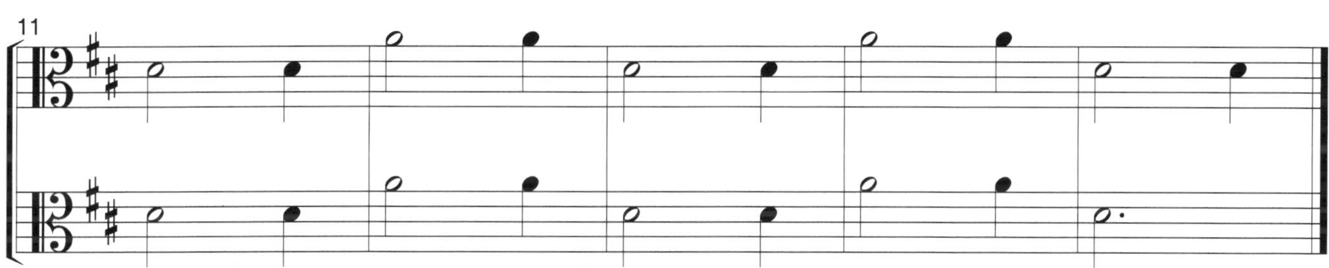

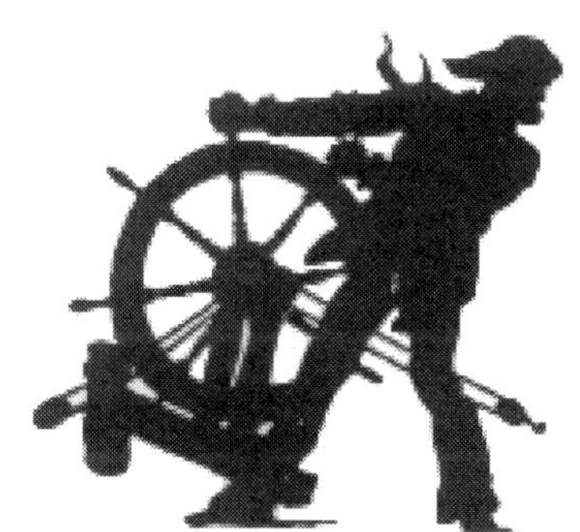

Come Again, Ho

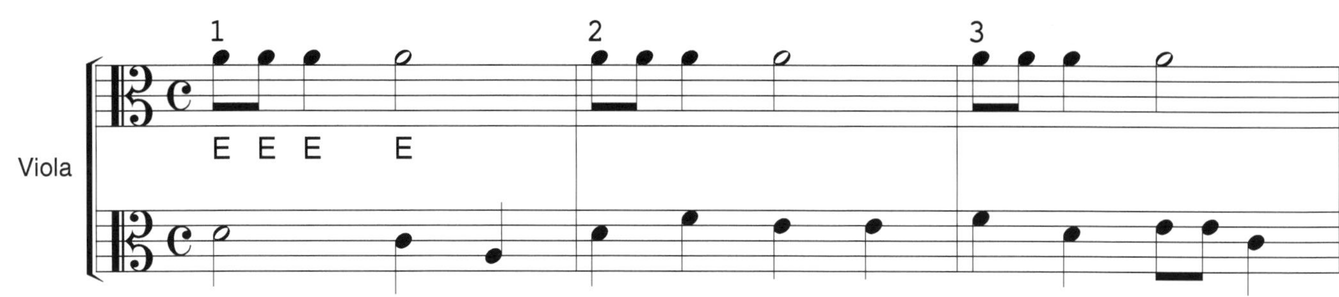

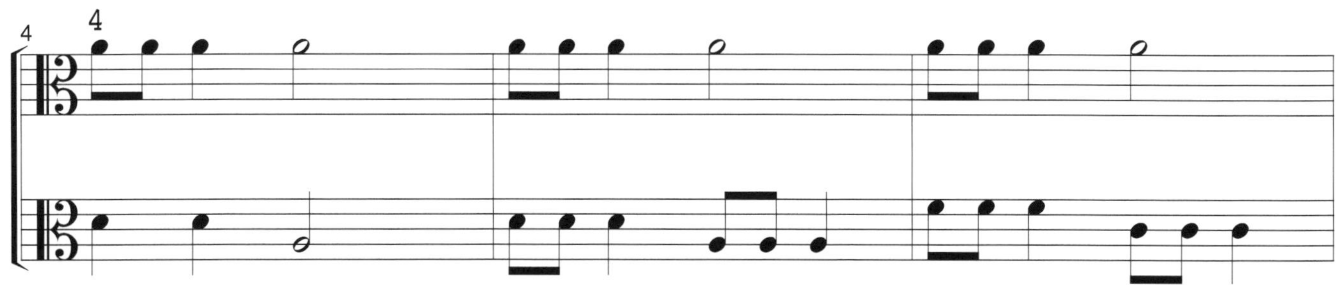

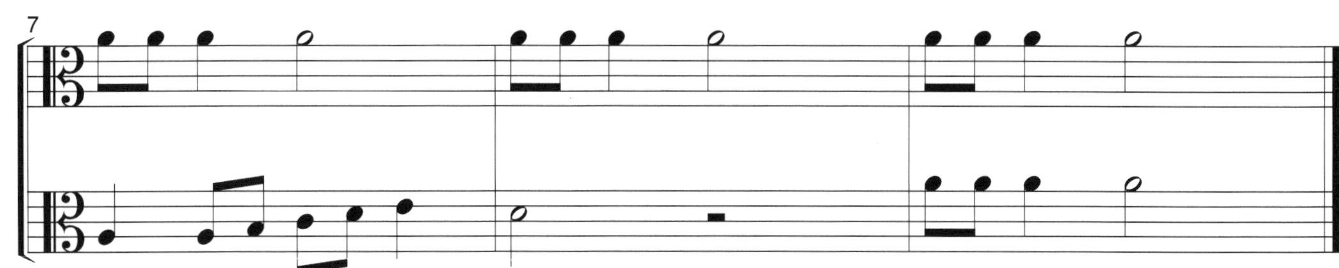

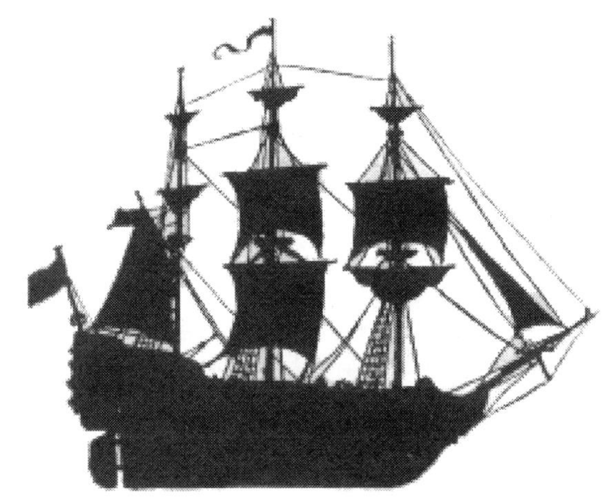

Nearly Done

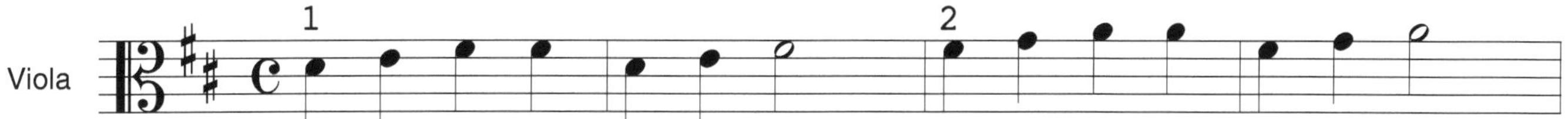
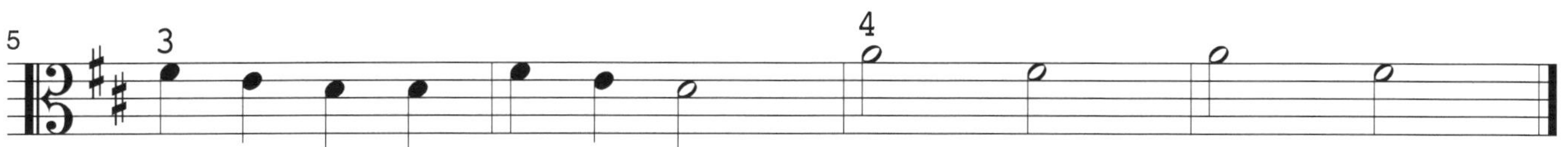

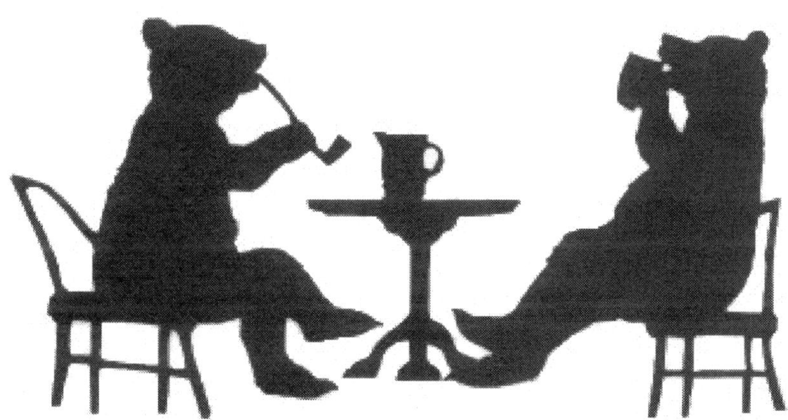

Alleluia, Amen

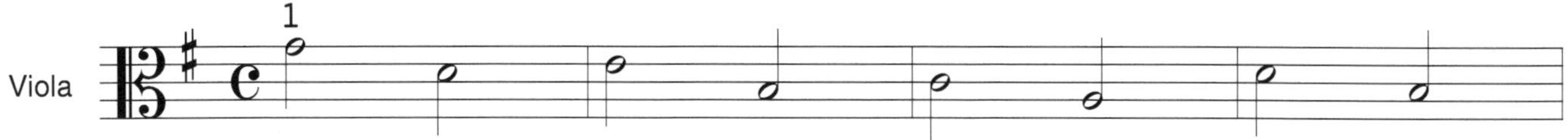

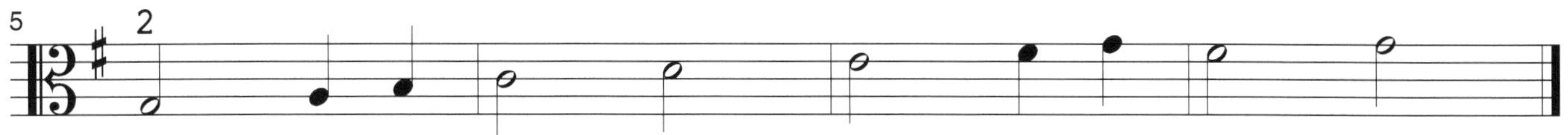

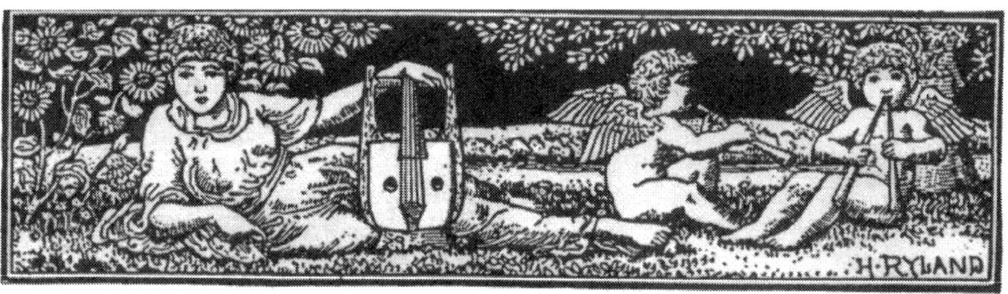

Dear Friend

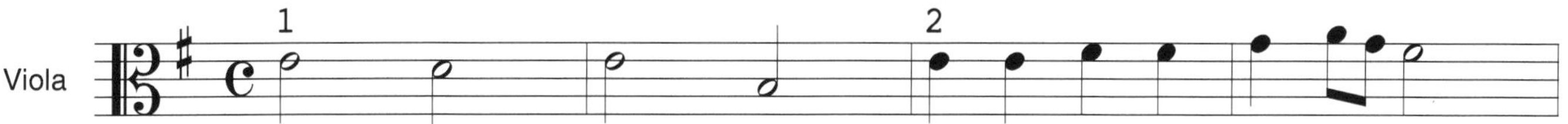

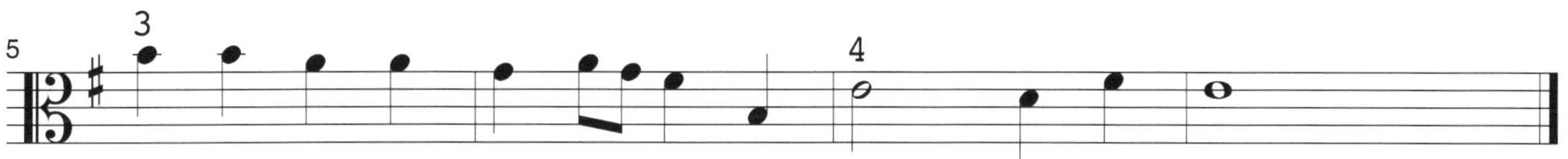

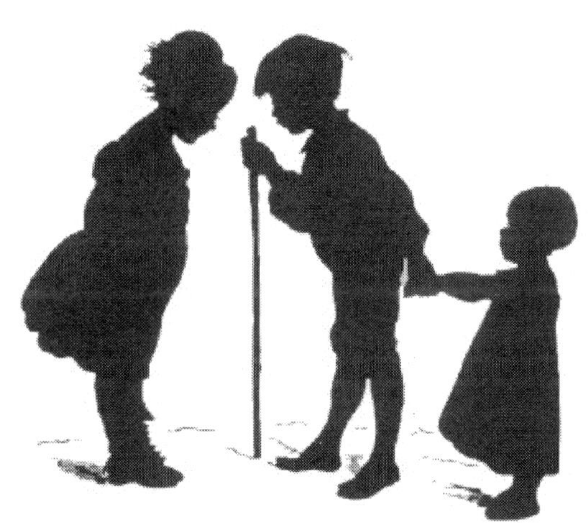

Viennese Musical Clock

Zoltan Kodaly

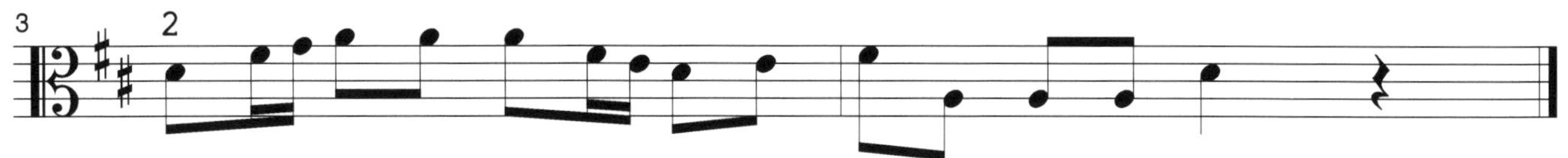

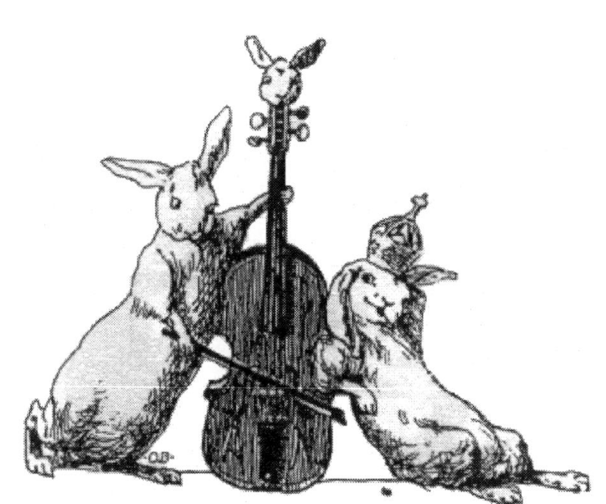

Shaker Life

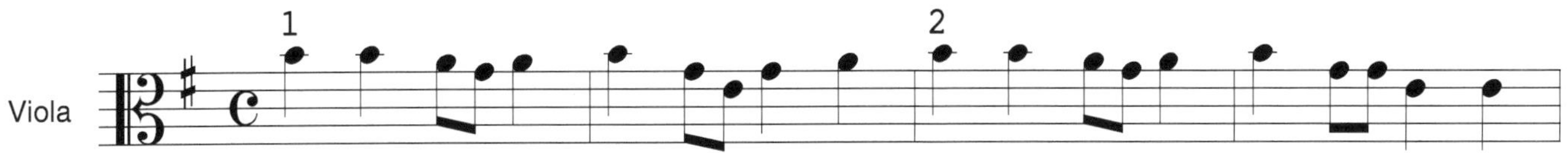

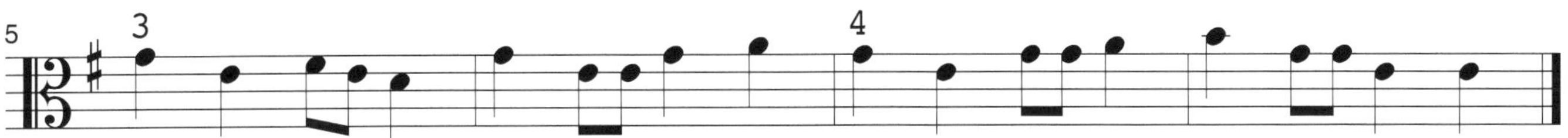

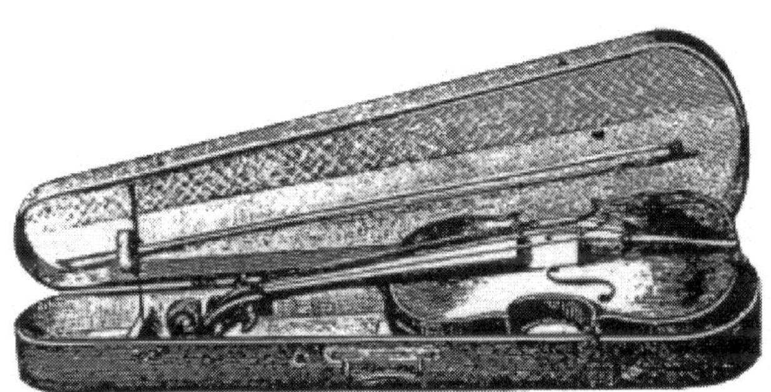

Vesper Round

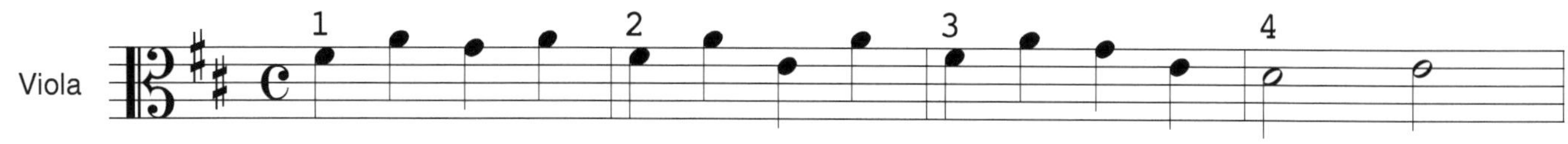

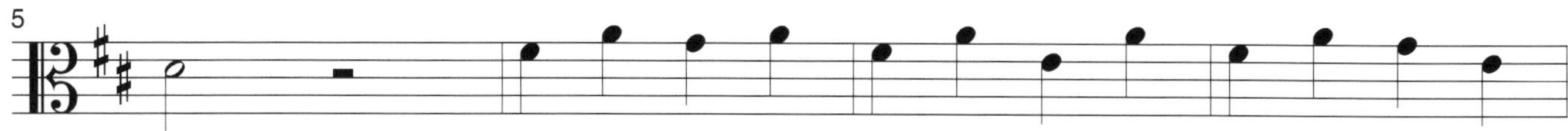

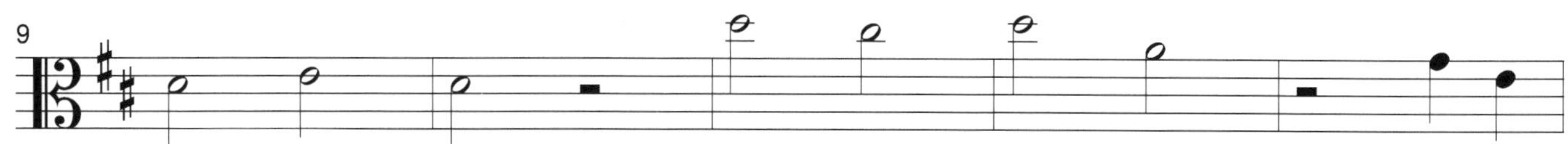

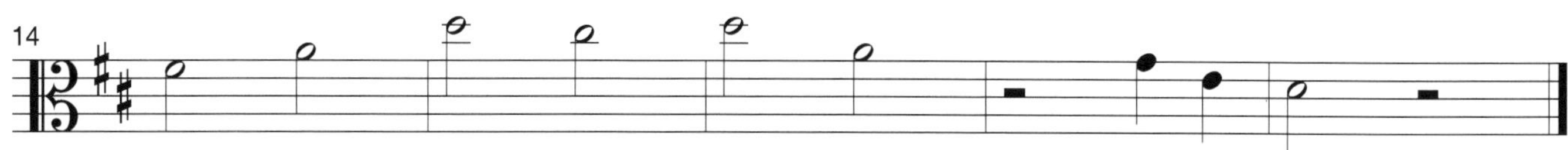

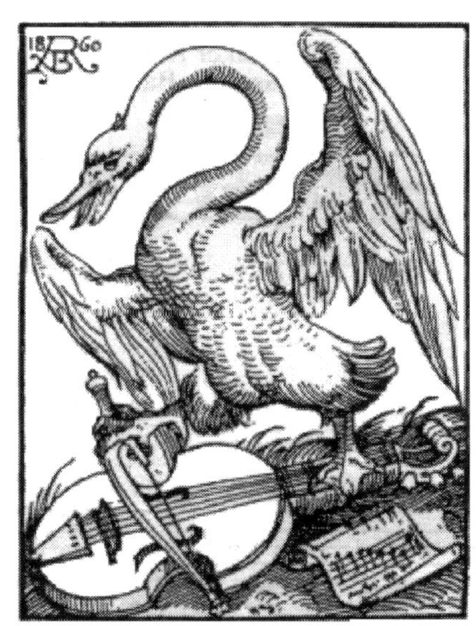

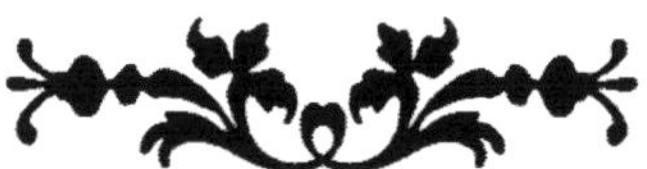

SOPHOMORE LEVEL
REPERTOIRE

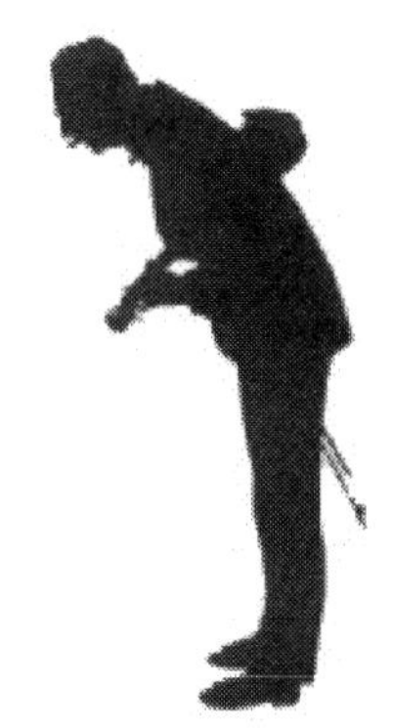

NEW NOTES:
LOW SECOND FINGER POSITION- FOURTH FINGER

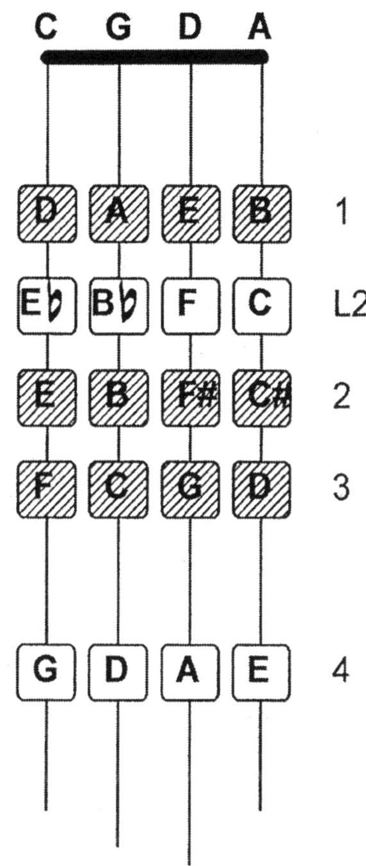

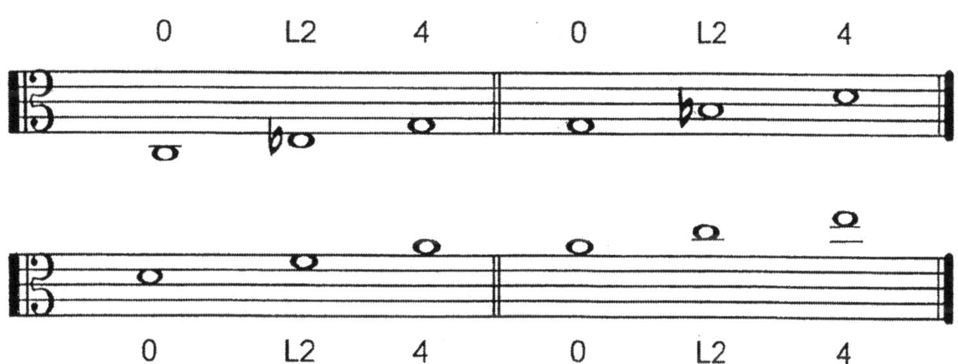

Come Again, Ho

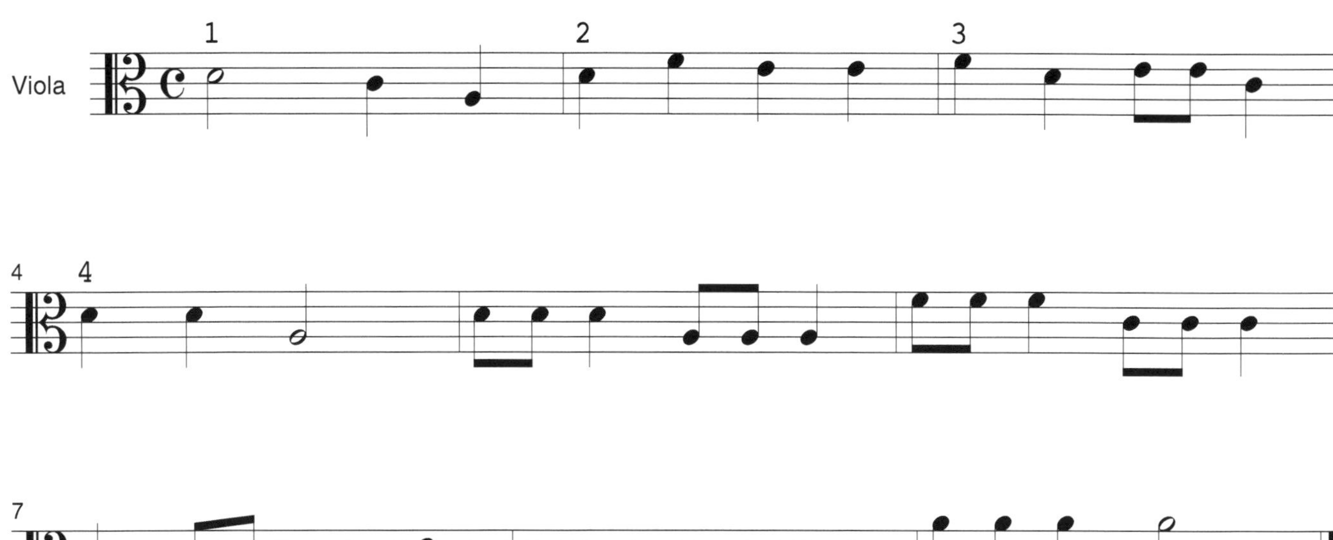

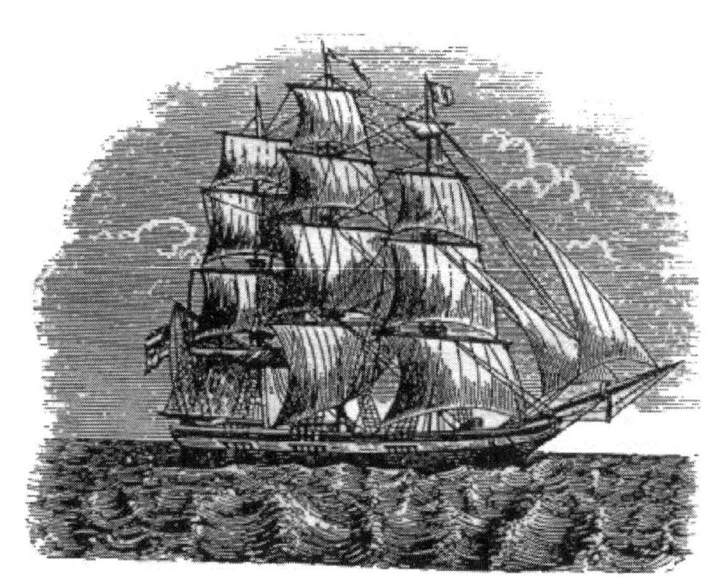

Oh, Music, Sweet Music

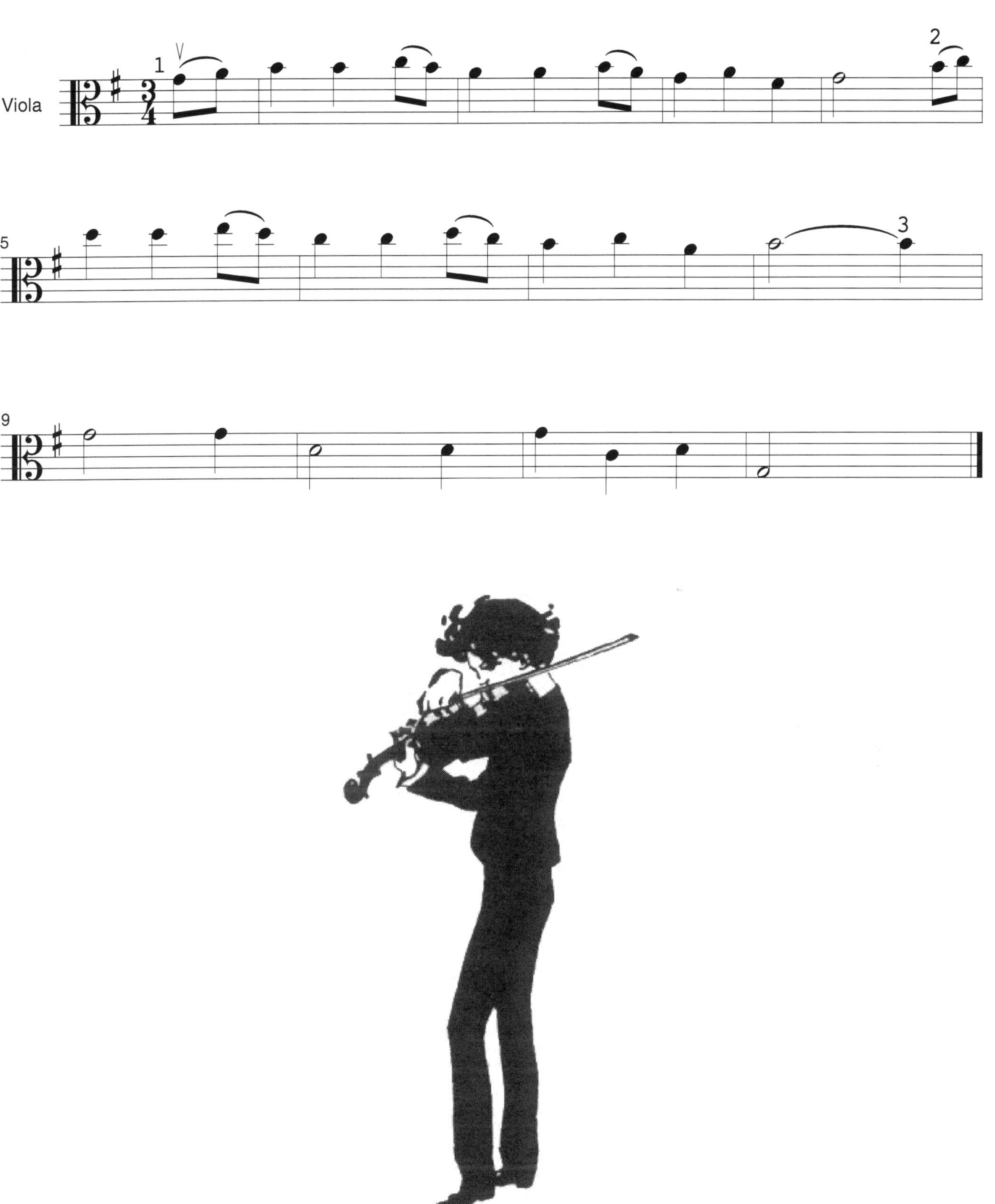

Hey Nonny No

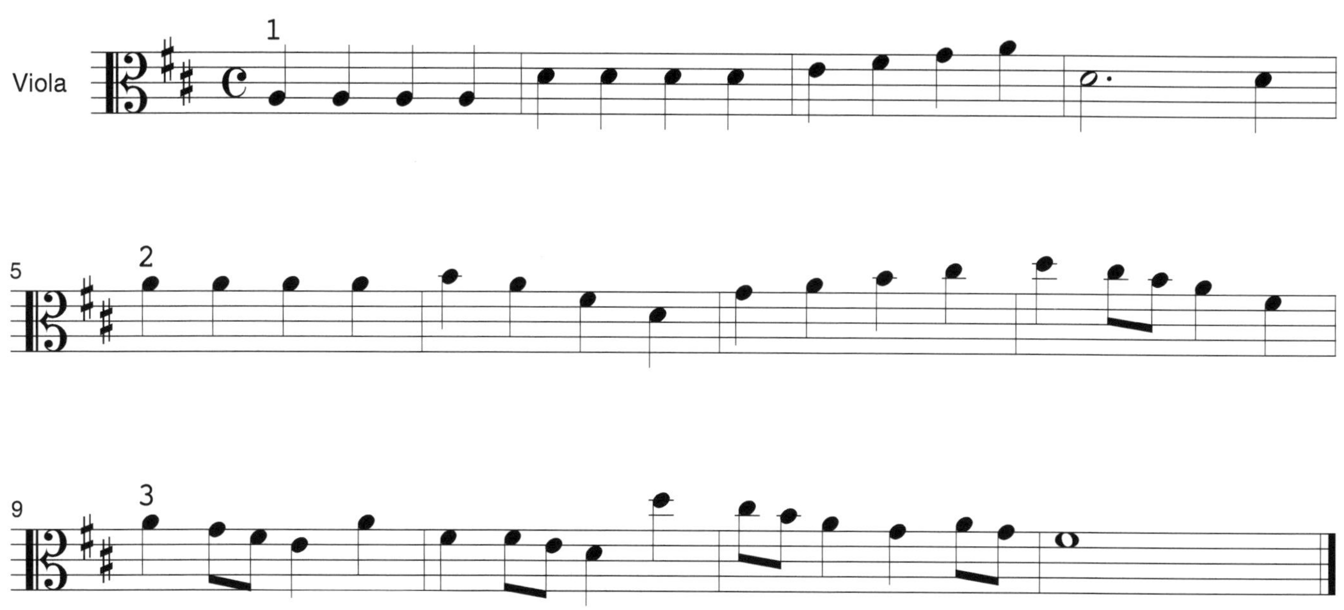

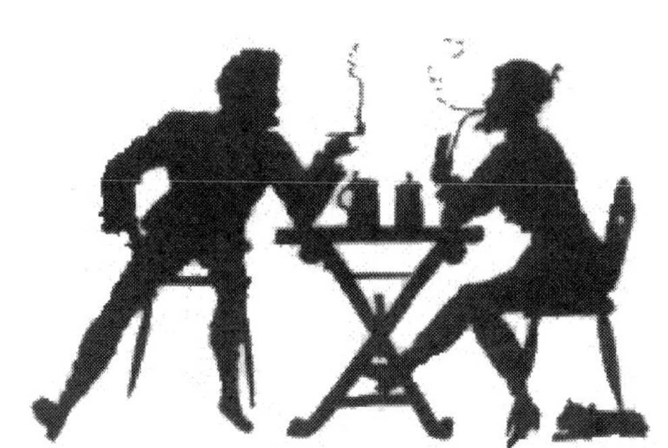

Peace and Plenty

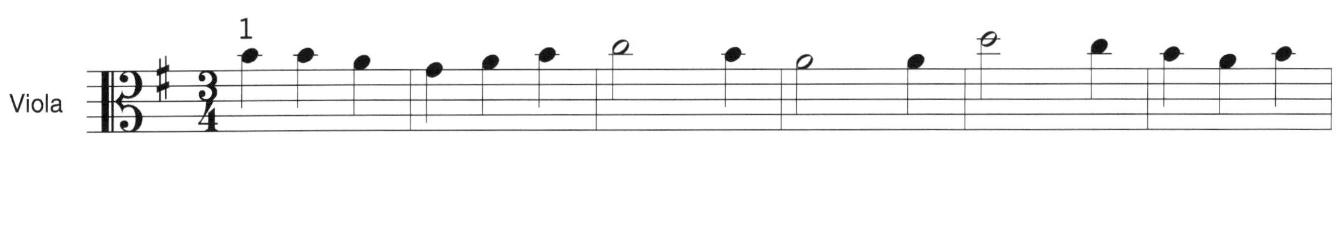

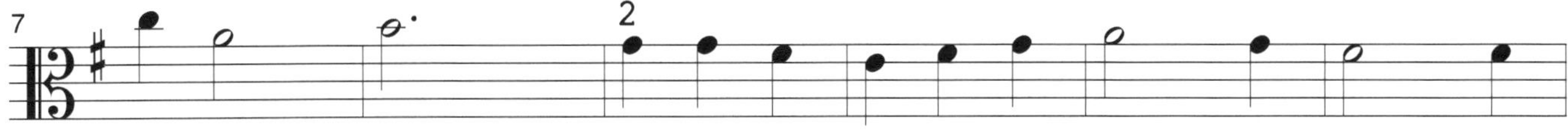

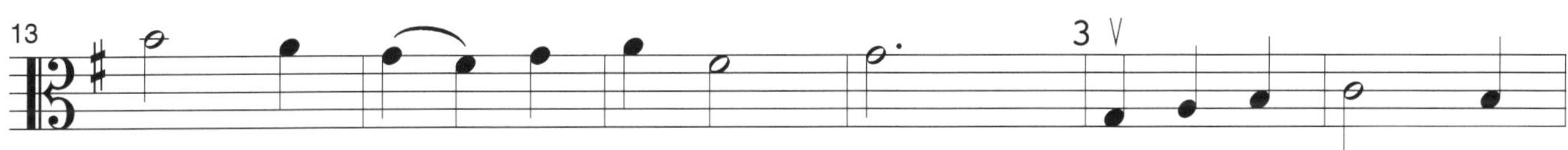

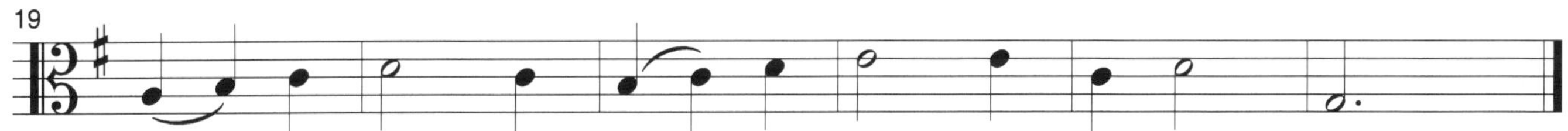

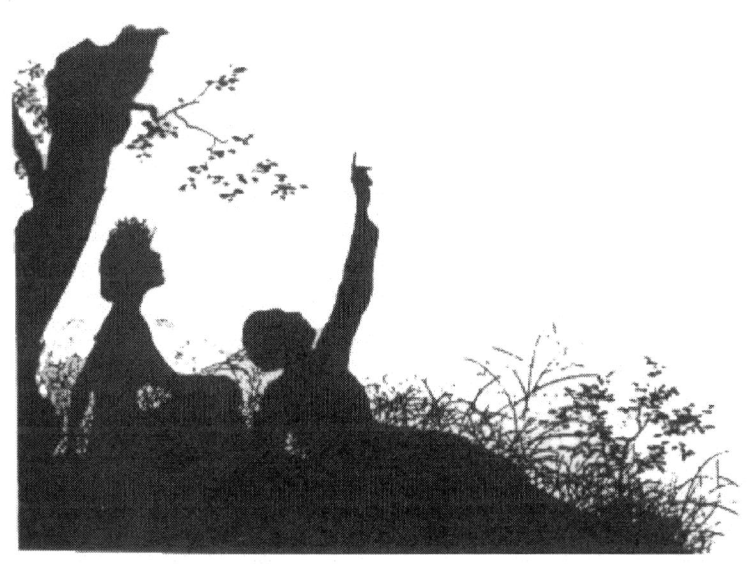

Good Hostess, Fill the Pot for Me

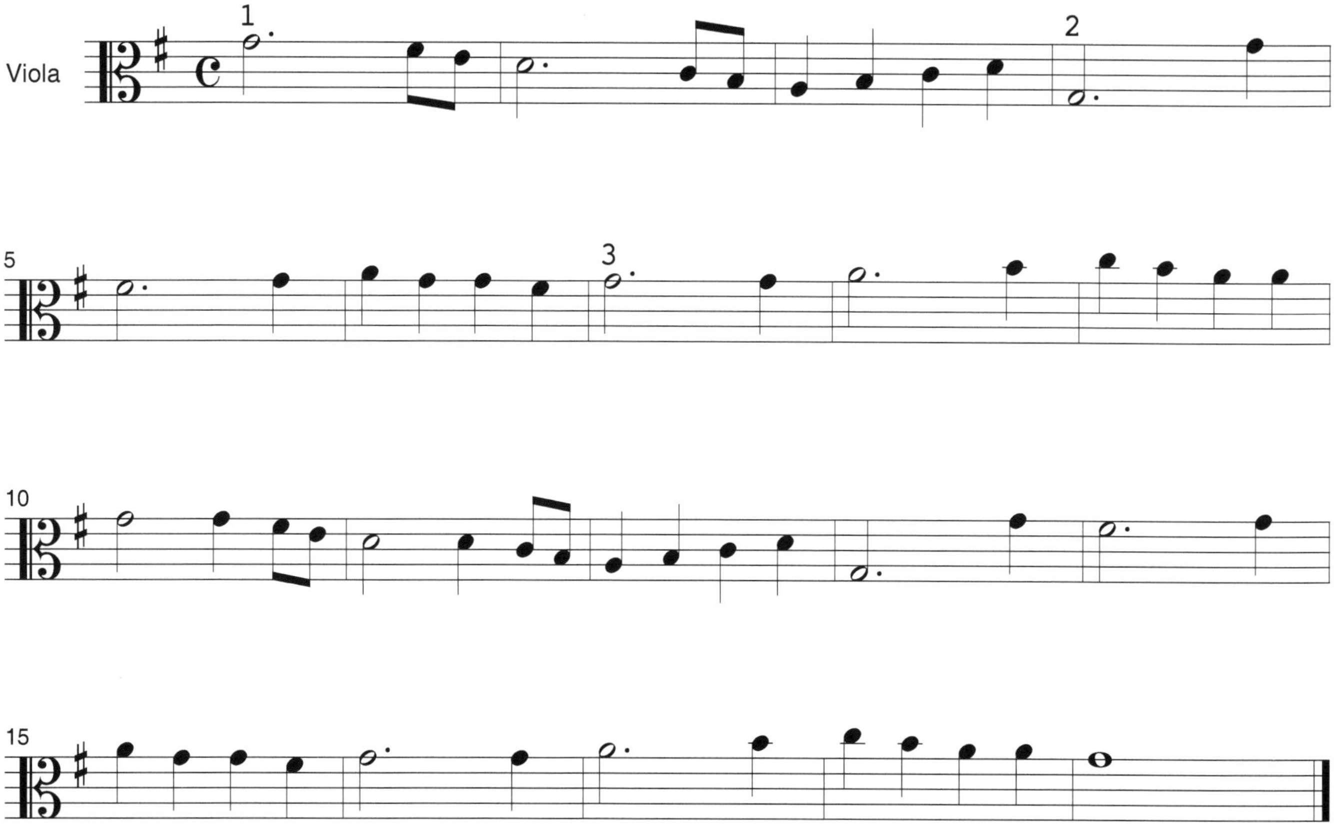

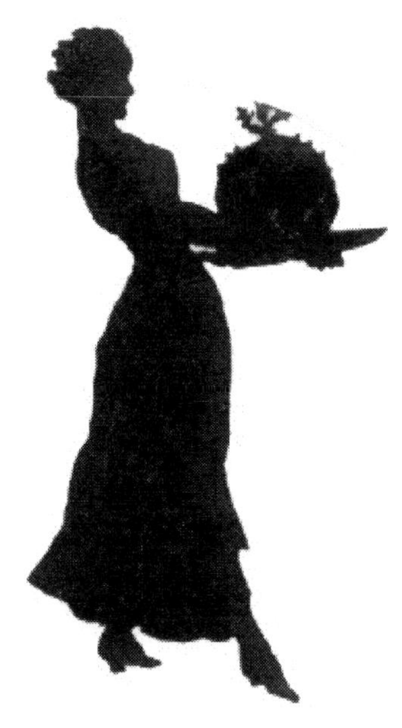

Invisible Fox

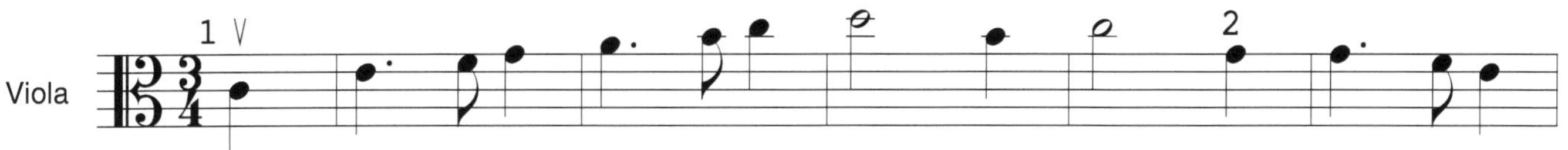

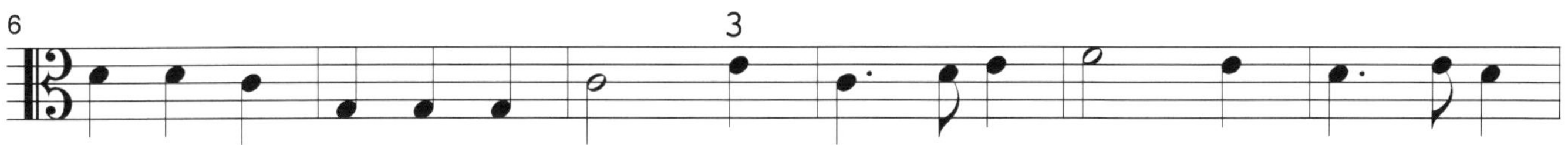

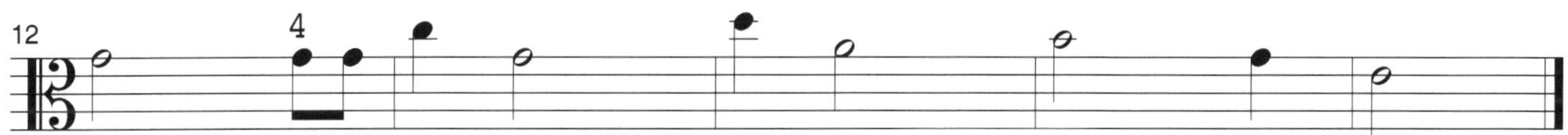

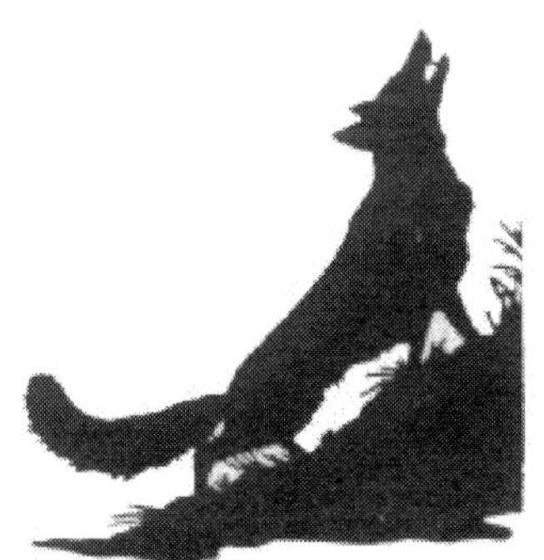

The Jolly Hunter

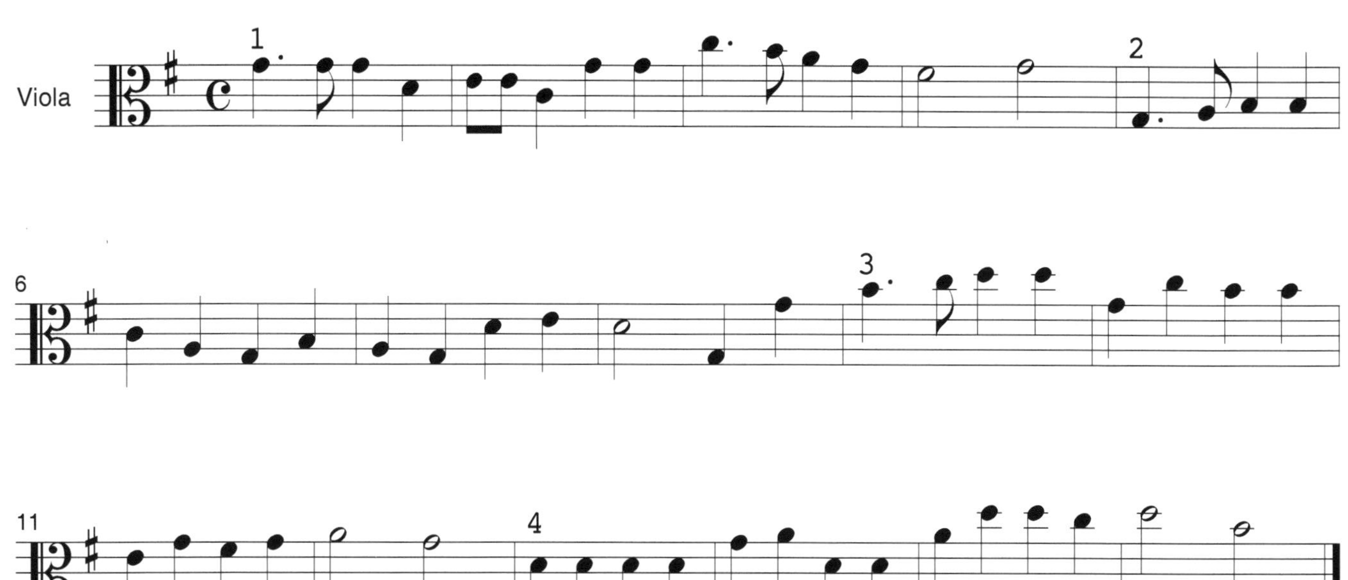

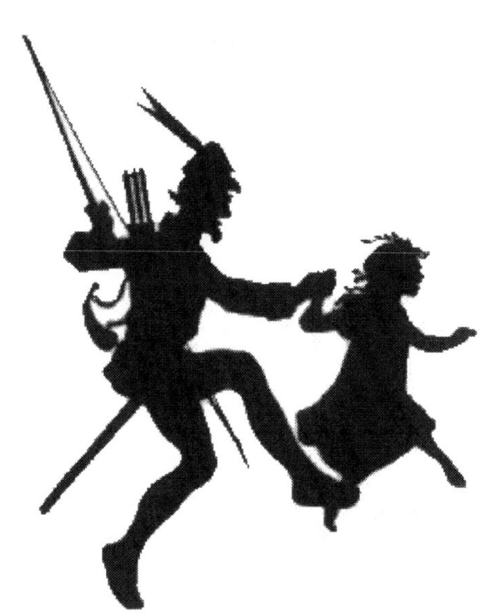

Si Cantemo

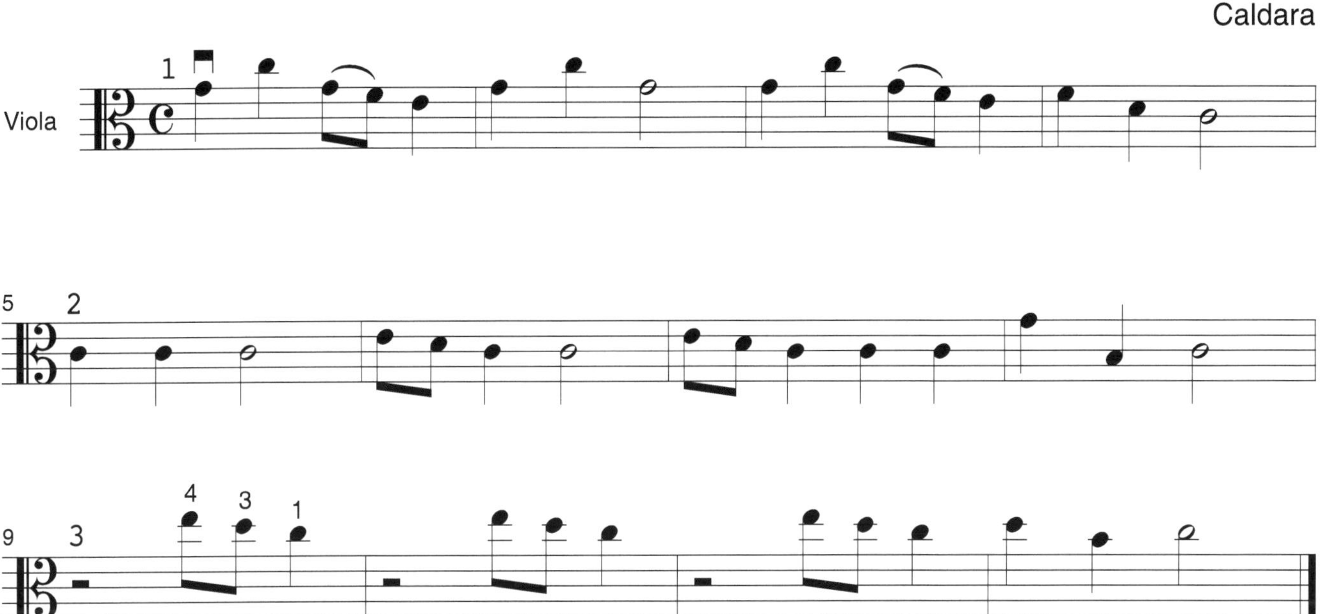

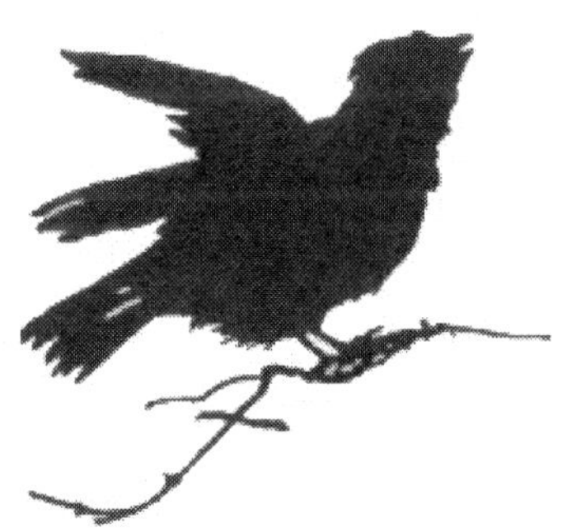

The Singing School

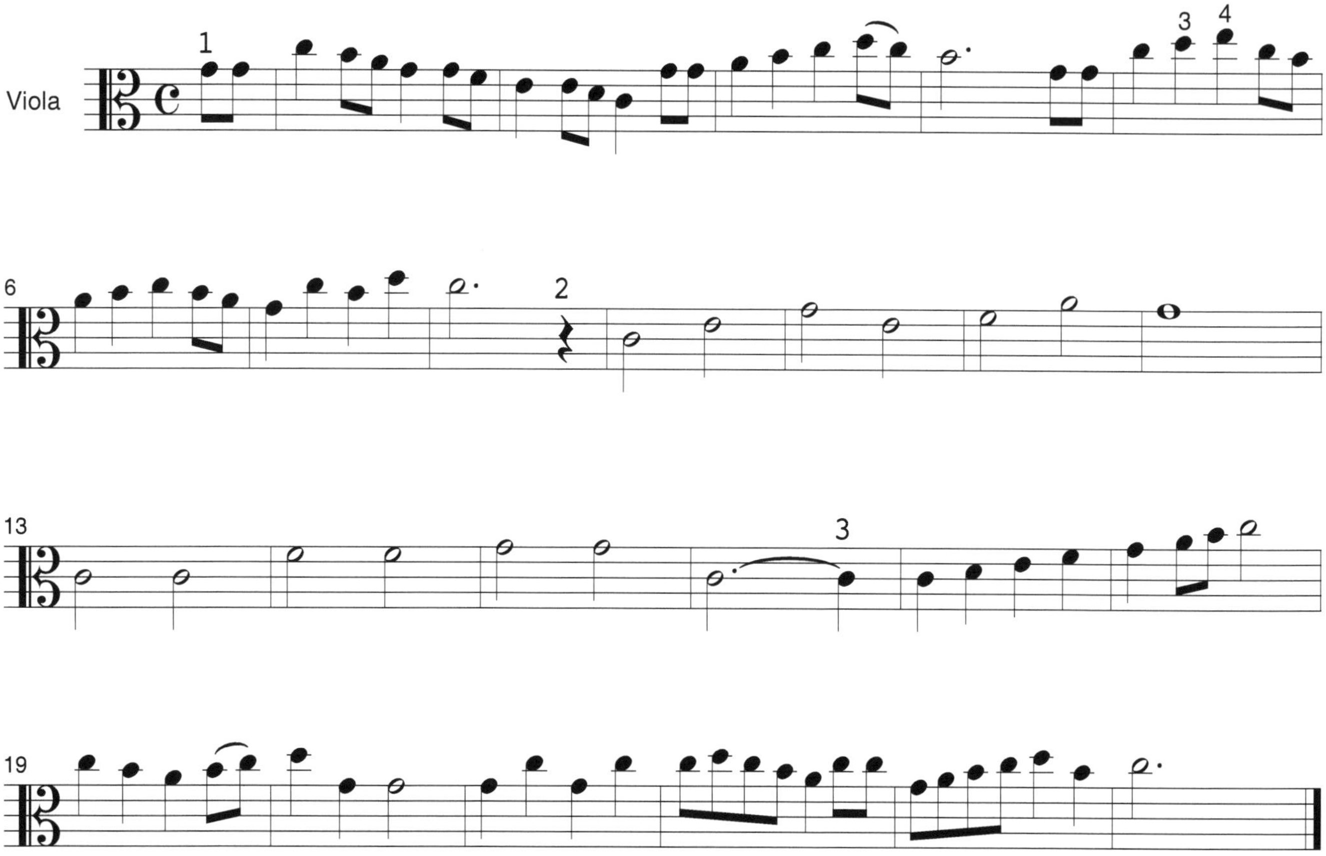

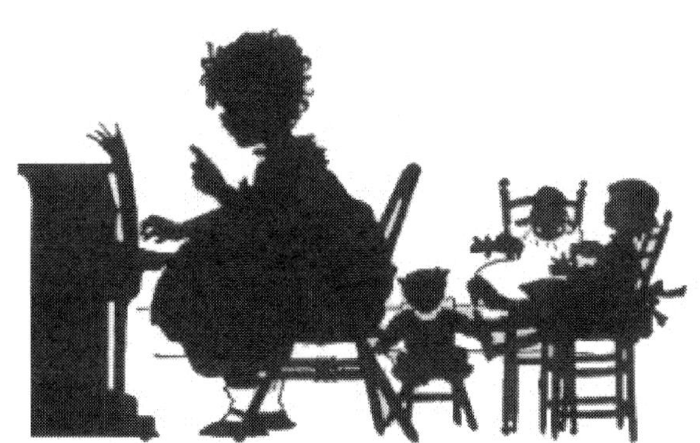

Shalom Chaverim

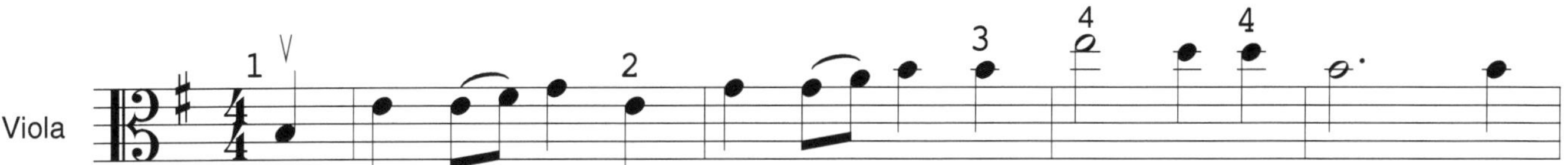

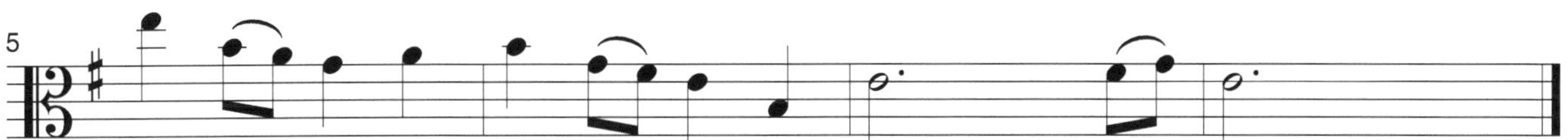

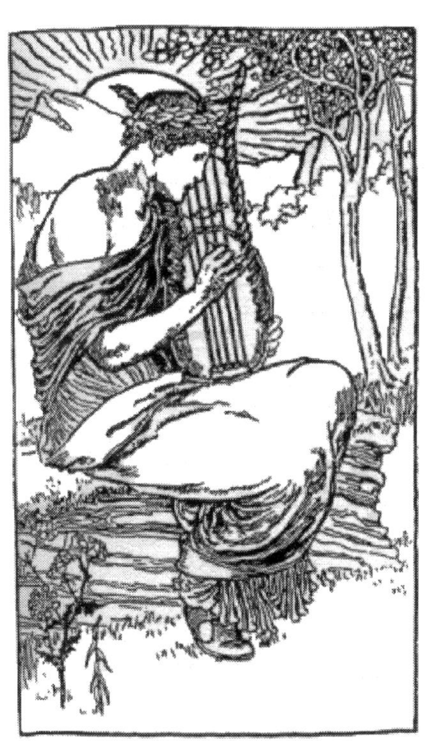

The Mighty Tom

Aldrich

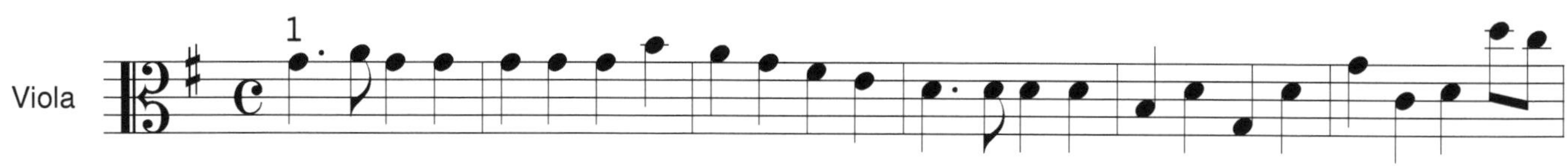

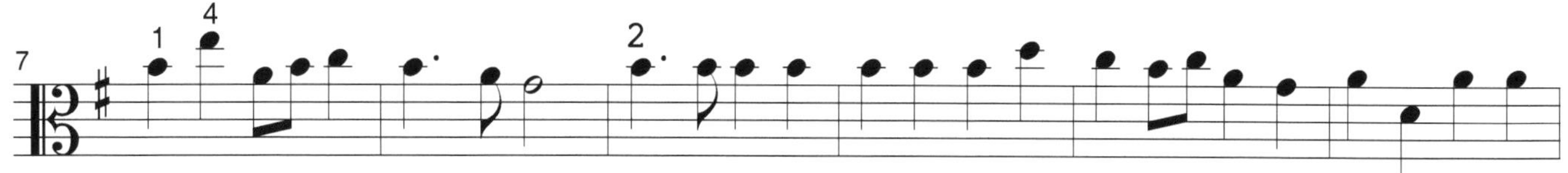

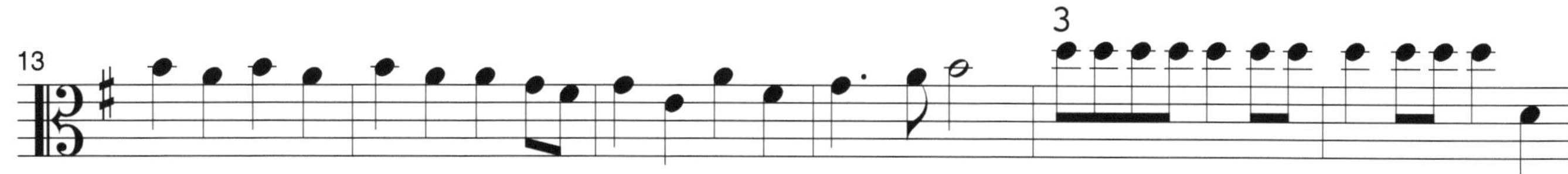

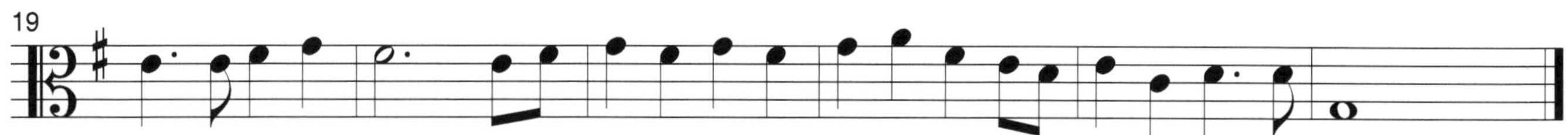

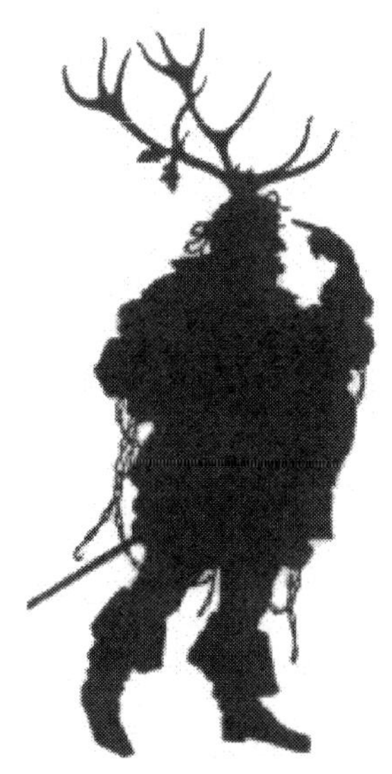

Echo Yodel Canon

(For Violas Alone)

Viola

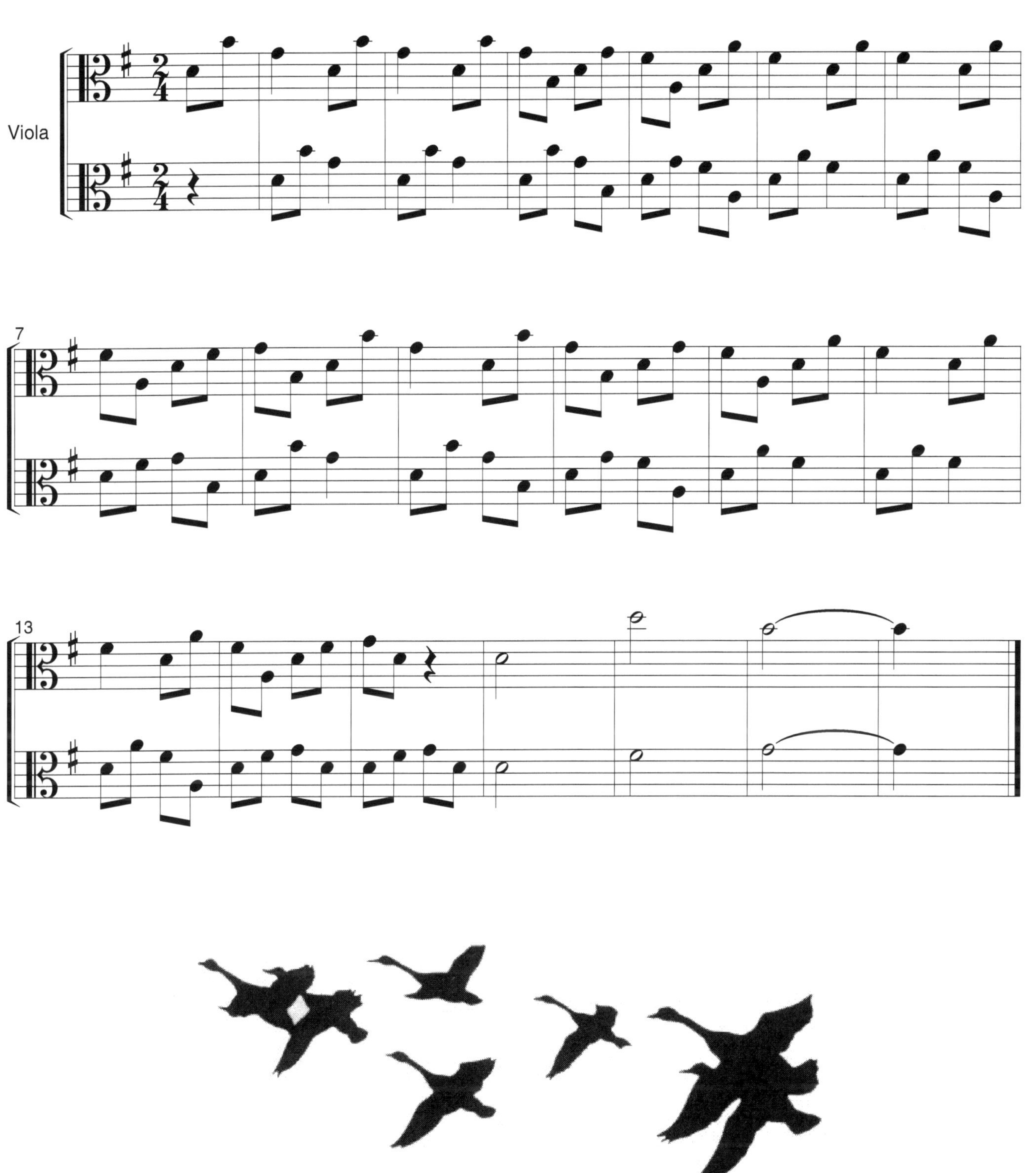

Orchestra

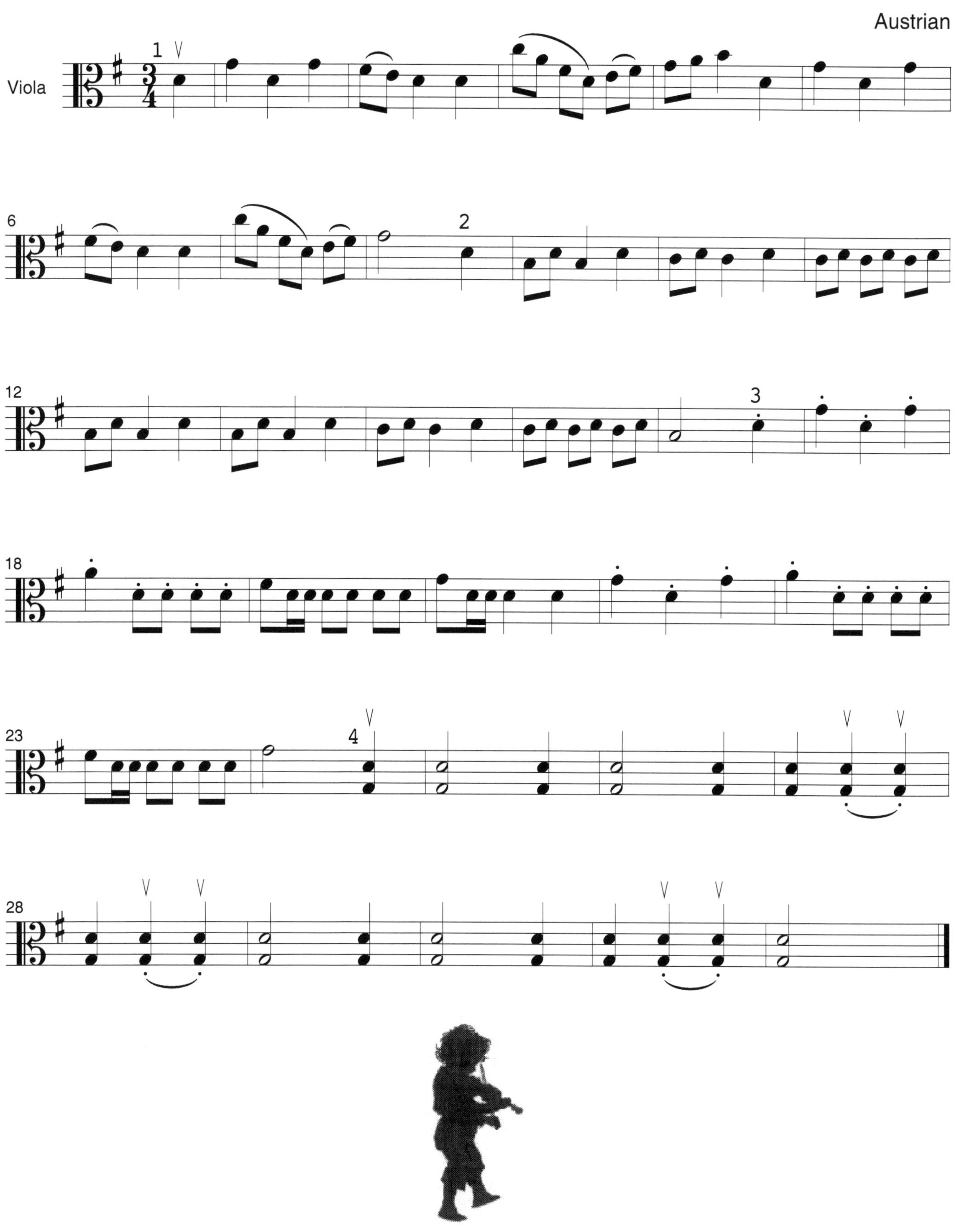

Reveille

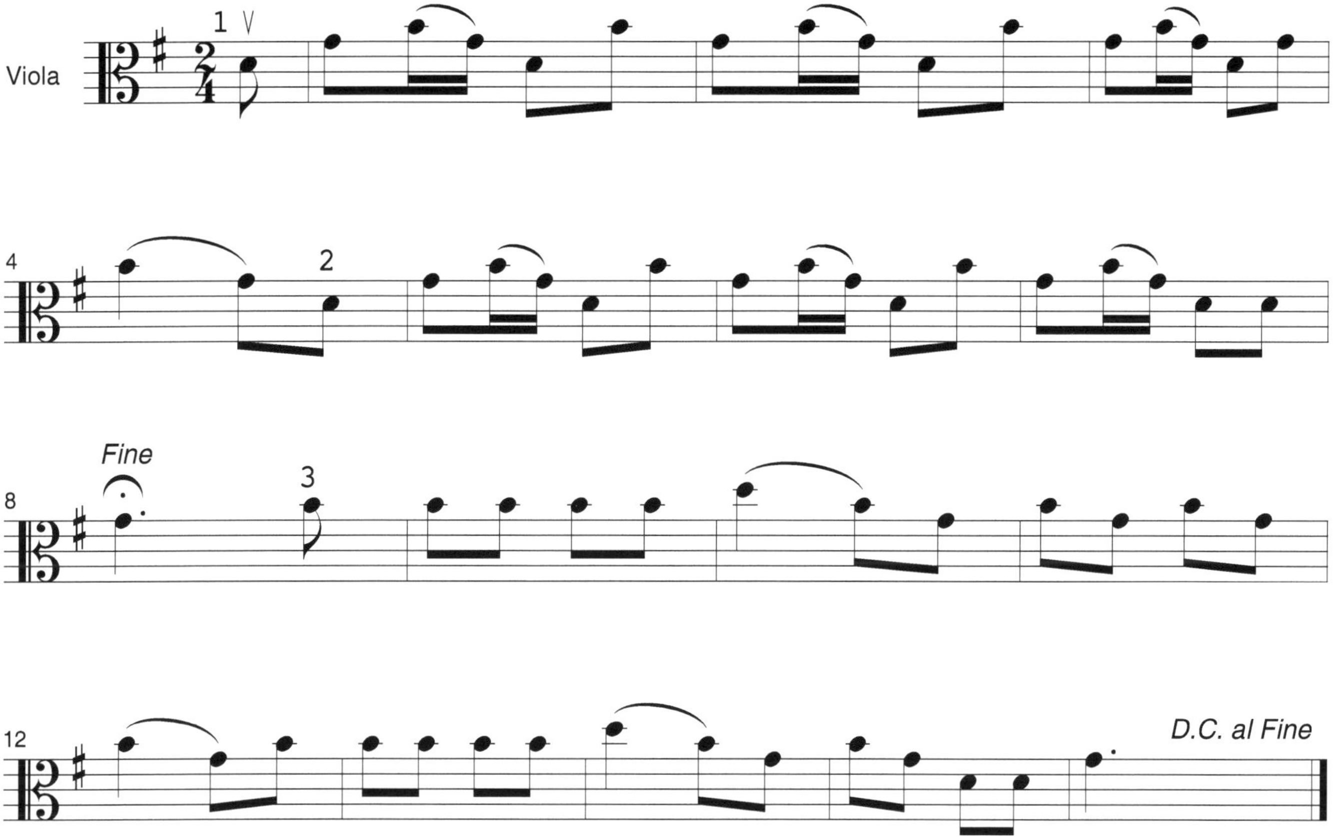

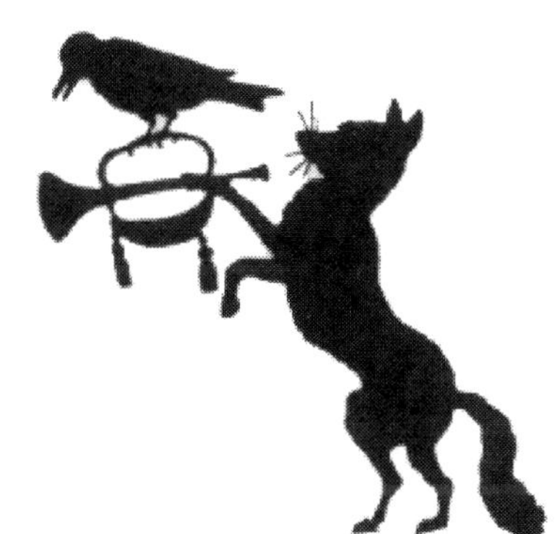

Merry Heart

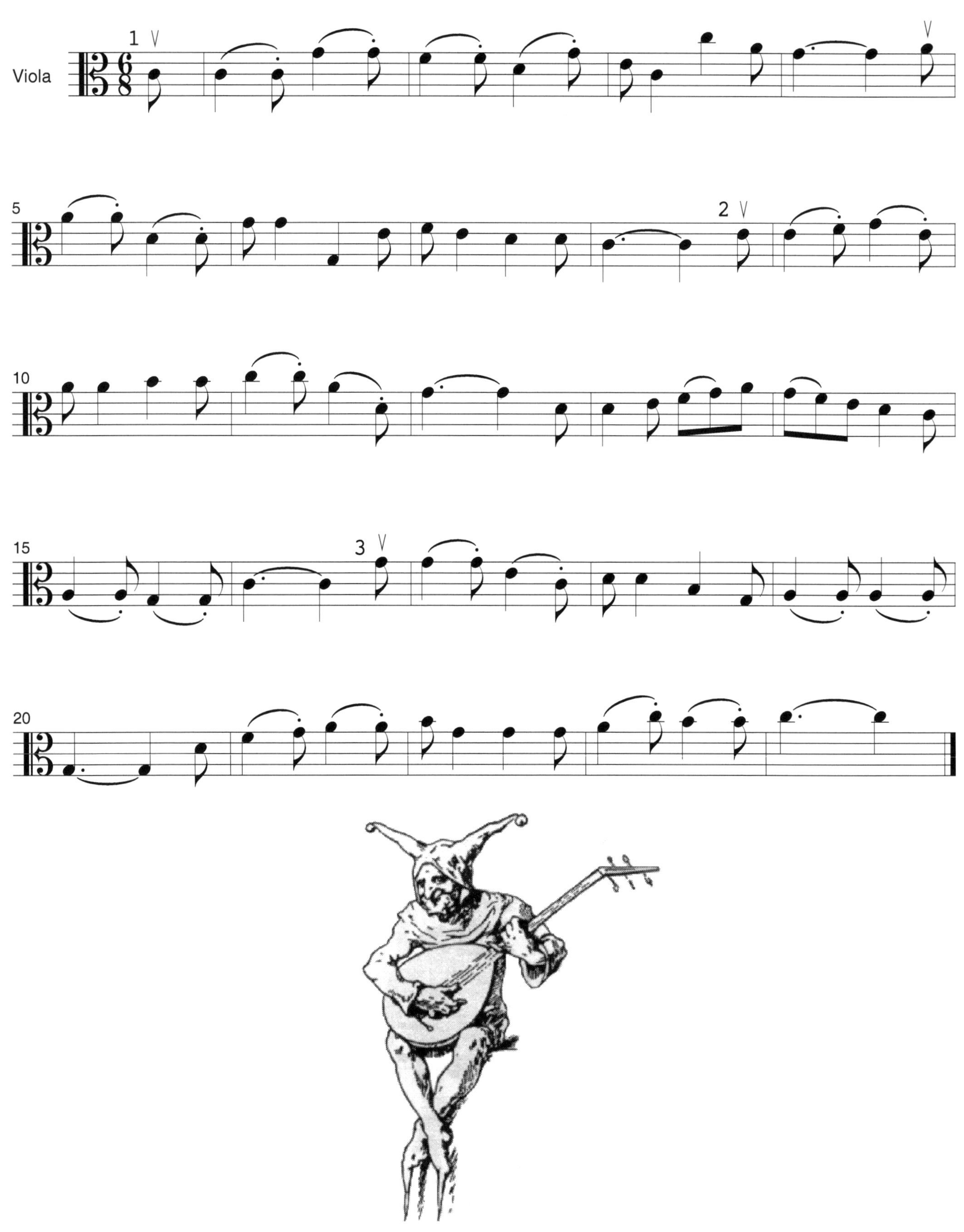

Dona Nobis Pacem

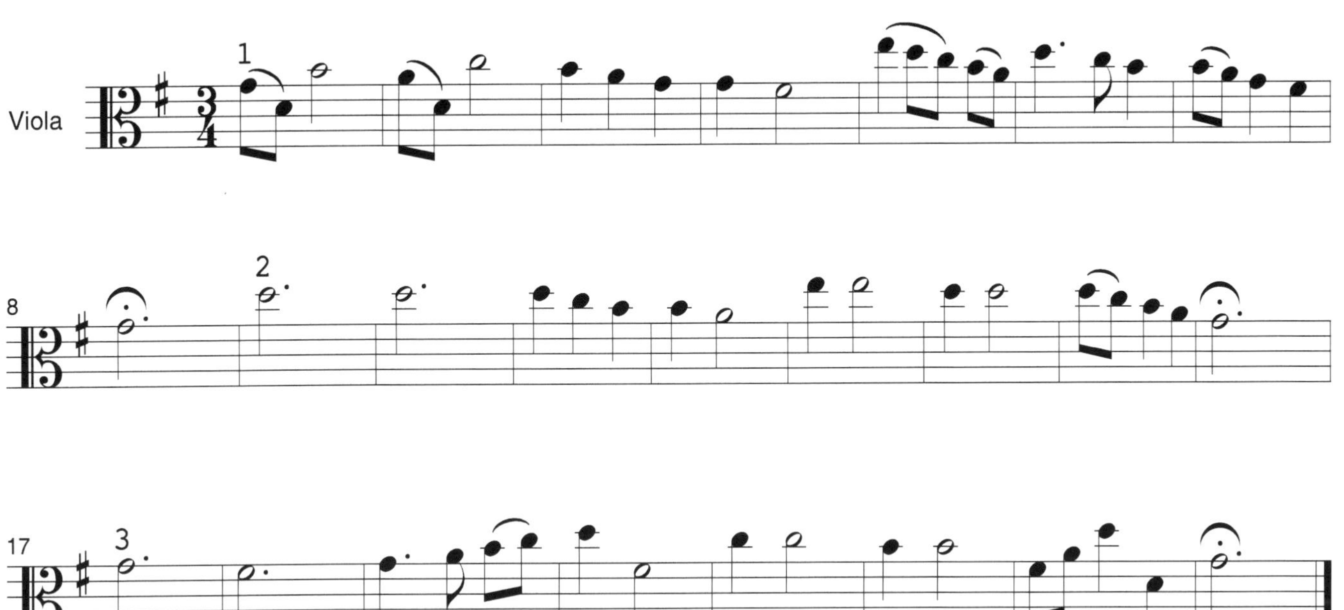

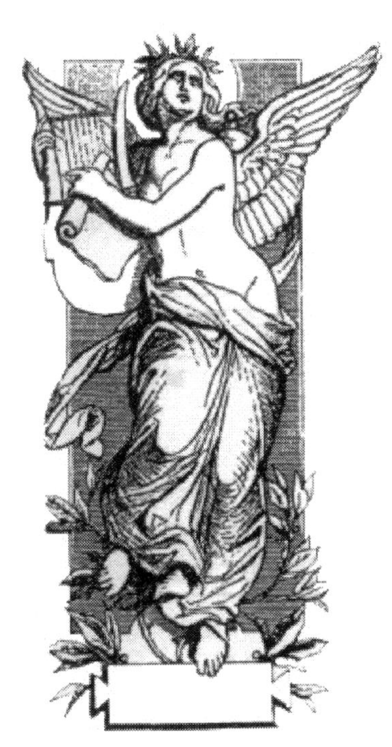

Round in G Major

Purcell

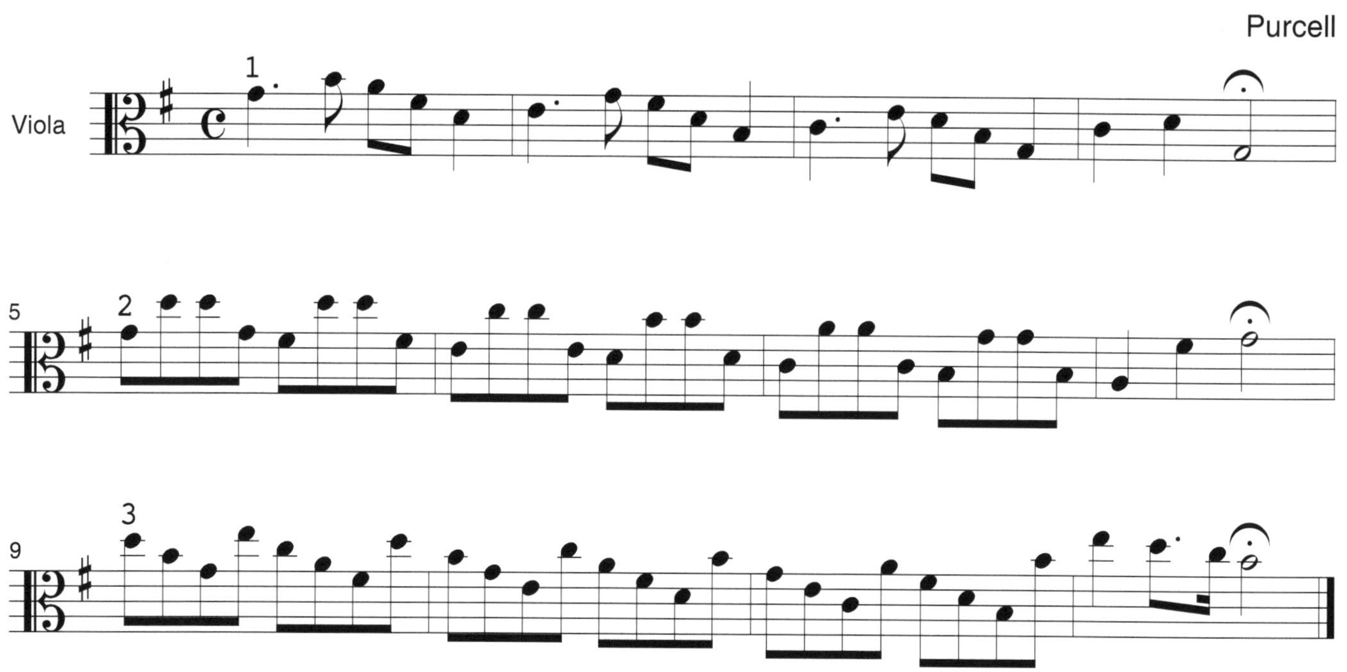

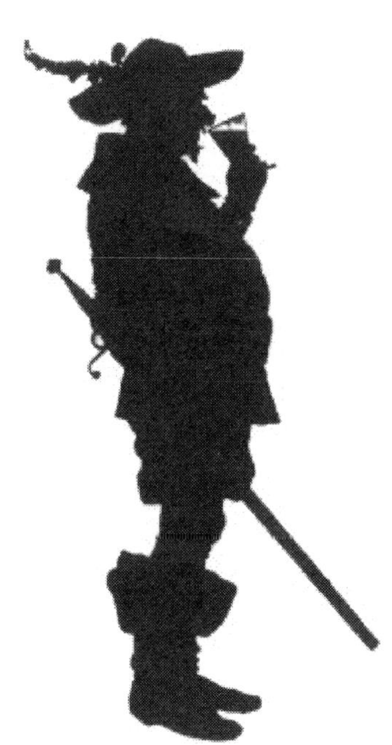

JUNIOR LEVEL
REPERTOIRE

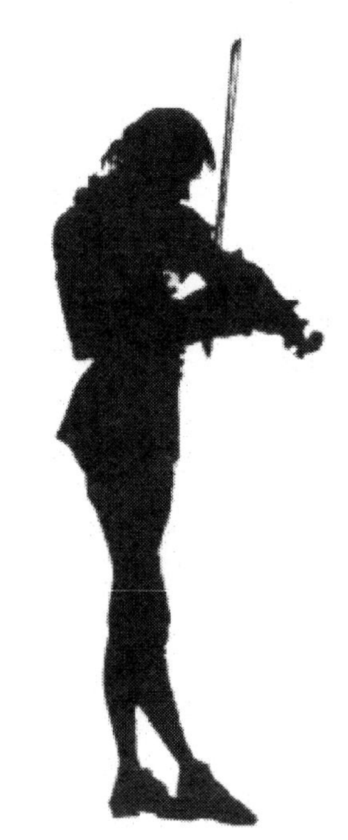

NEW NOTES
HIGH THIRD FINGER POSITION-
LOW FIRST FINGER POSITION-

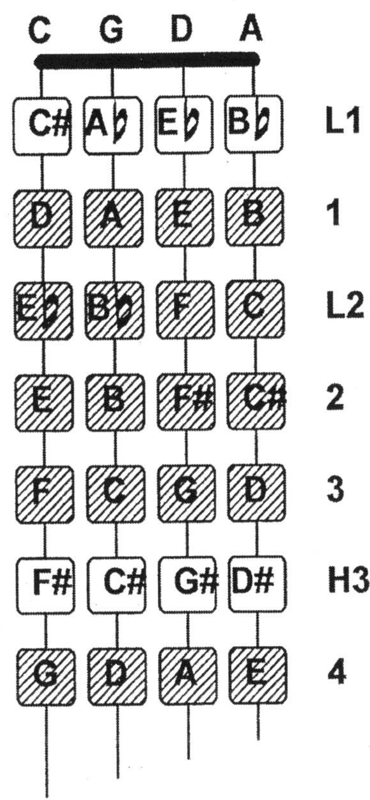

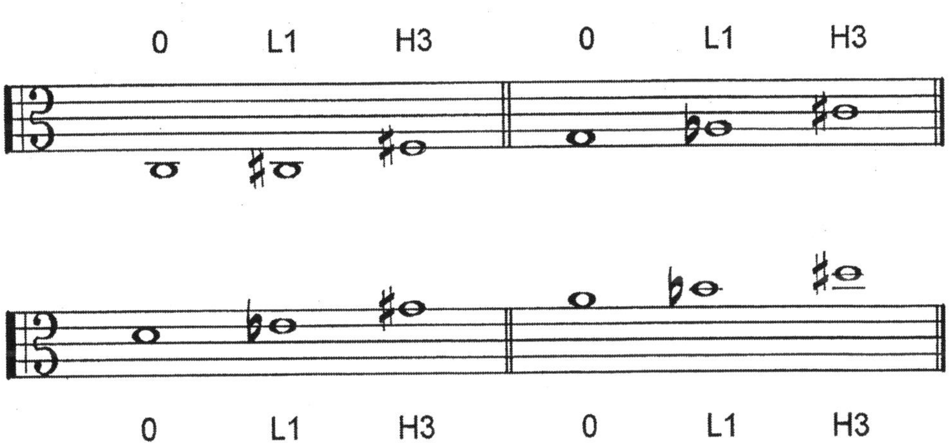

Rose

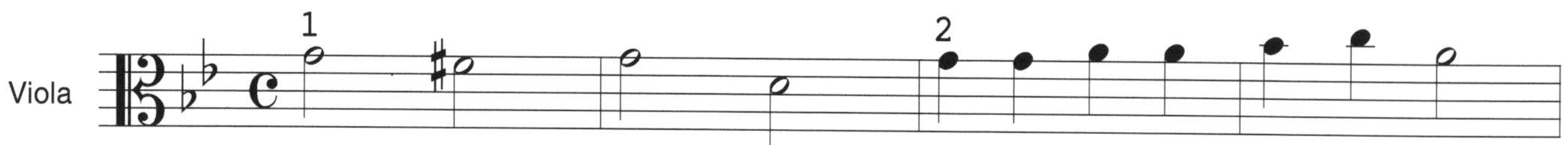

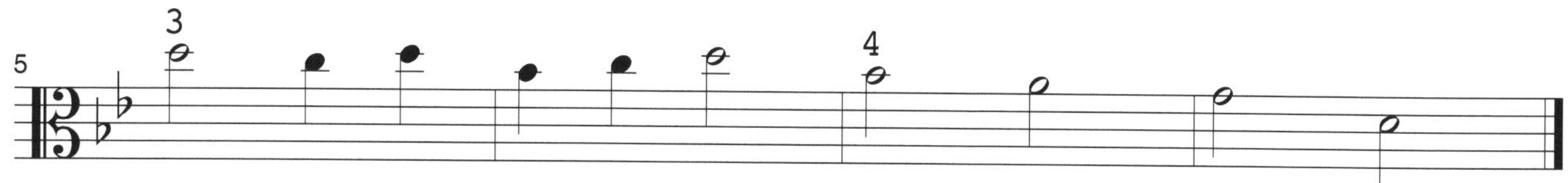

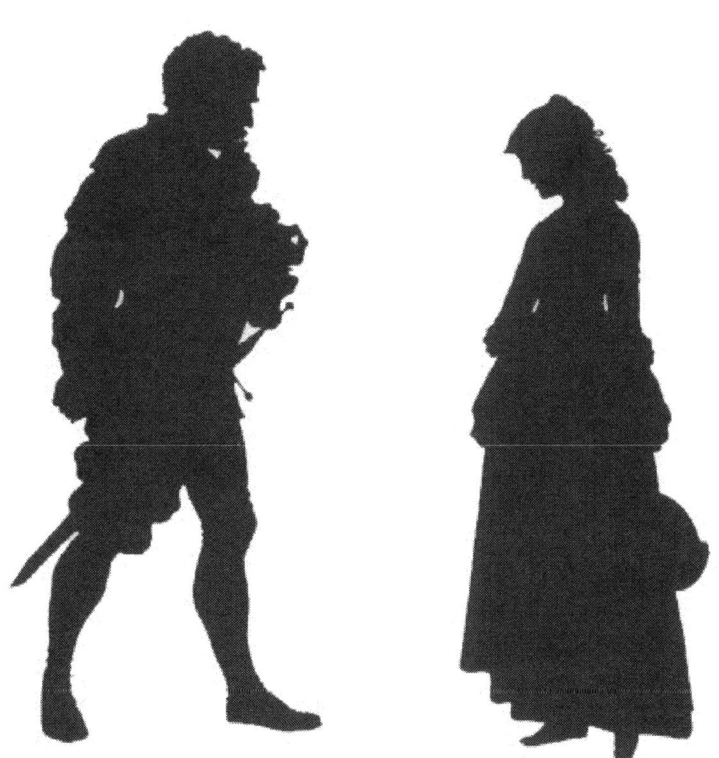

Just Teasing

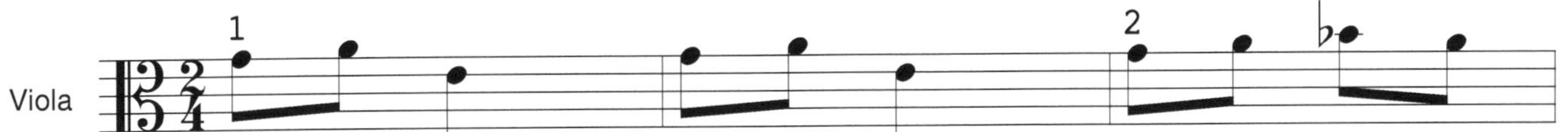
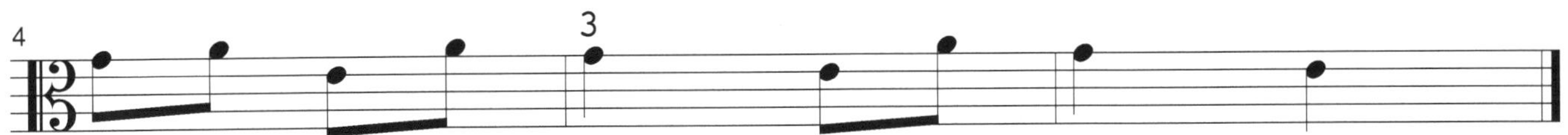

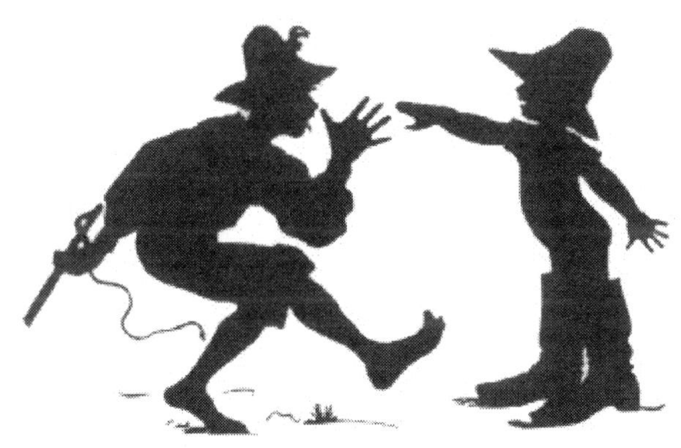

Heigh, Ho, Anybody Home?

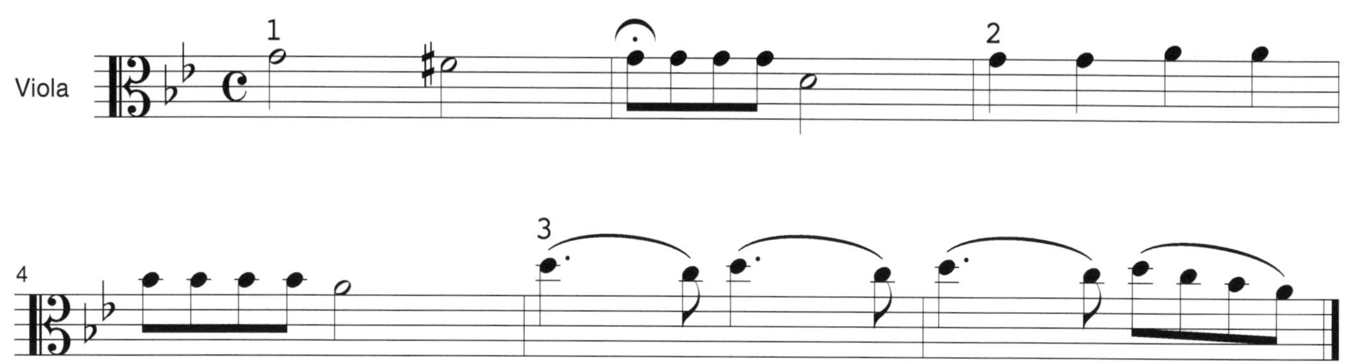

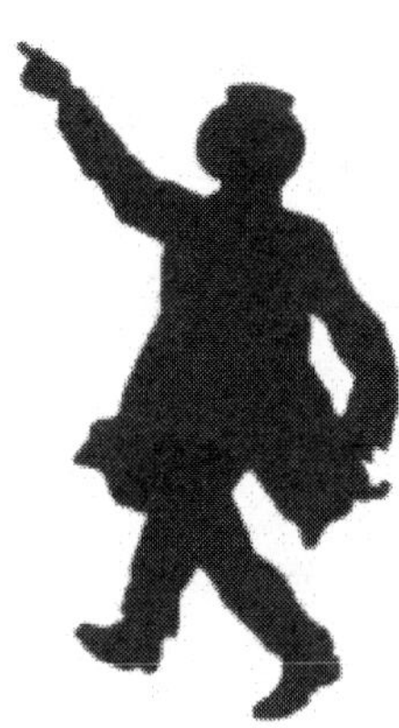

Let Us Sing Together

Czechoslovakian

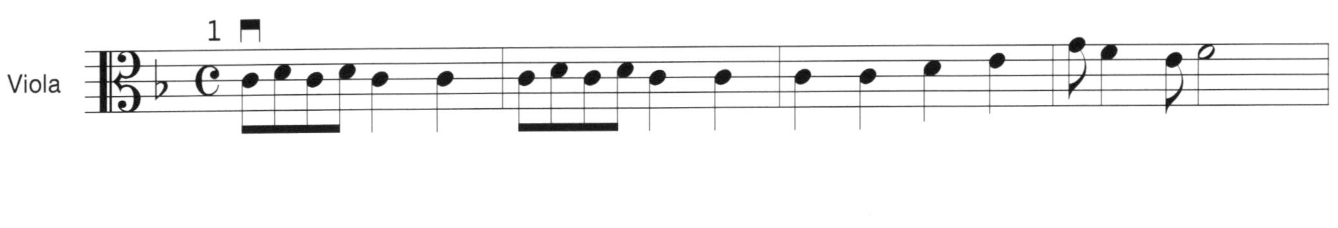

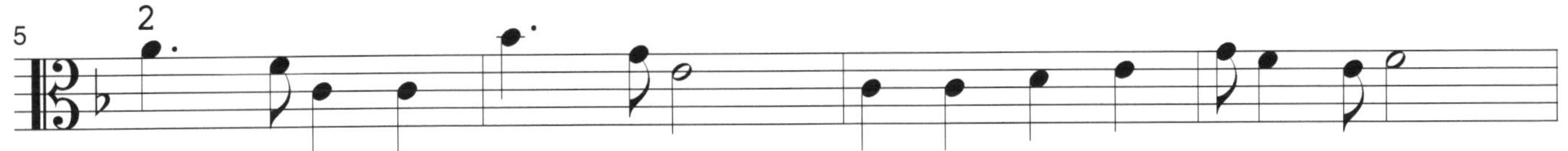

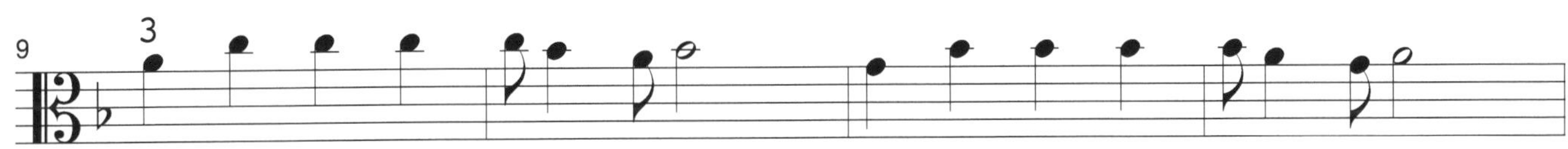

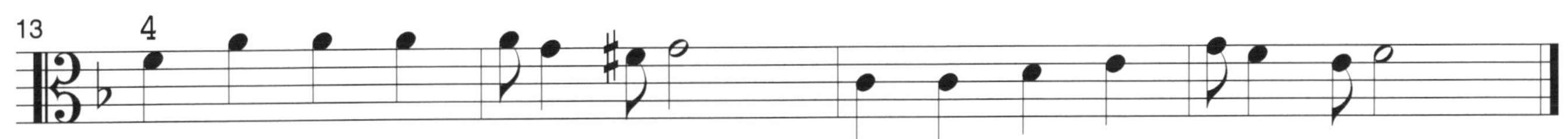

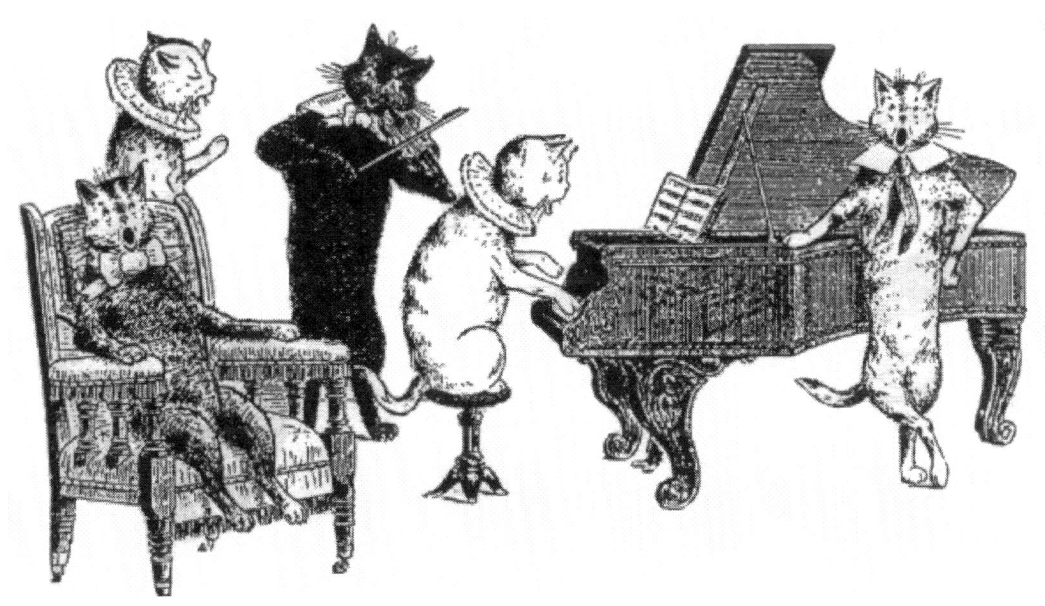

Sleep, Baby, Sleep

Johannes Brahms
Opus 113

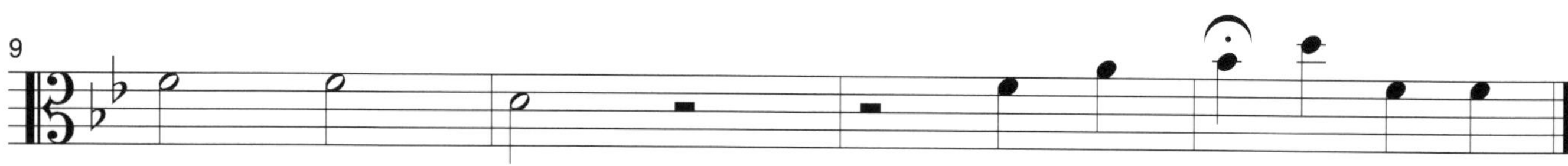

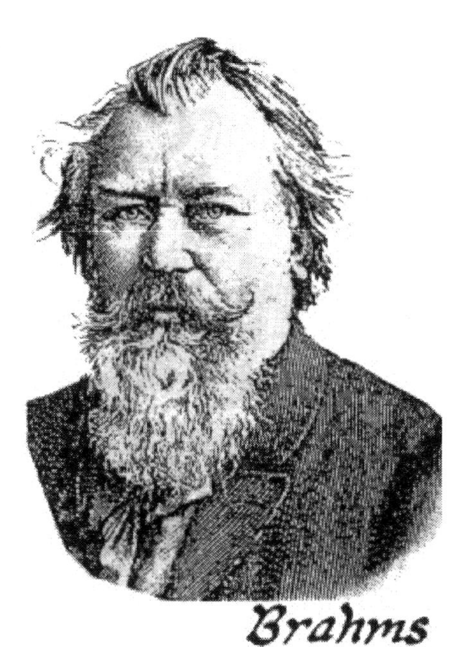

The Oriole Canon

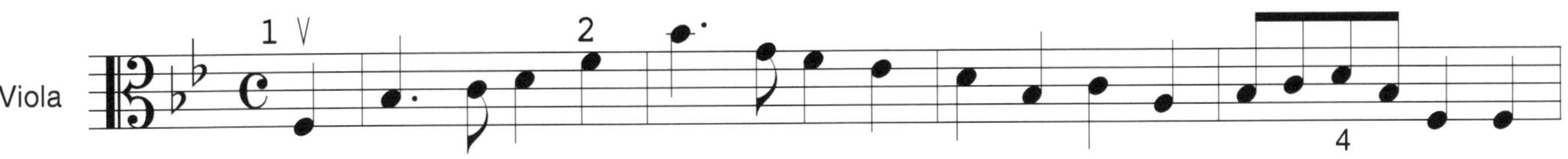

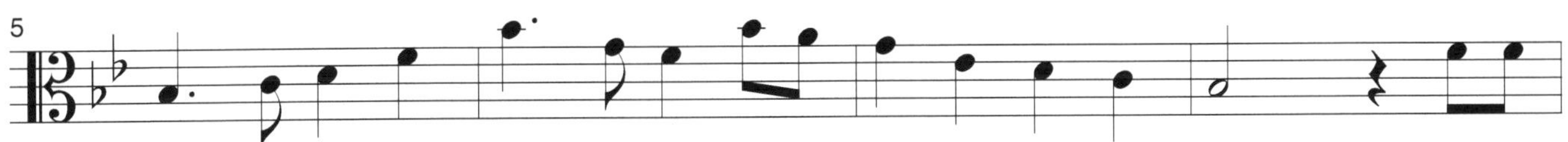

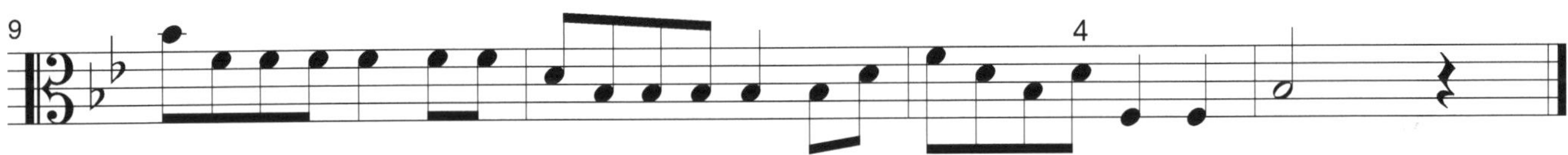

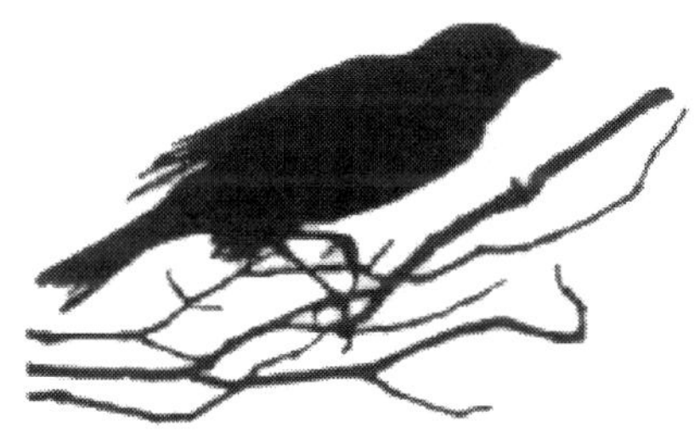

(For Viola Alone)

Who'll Buy My Roses?

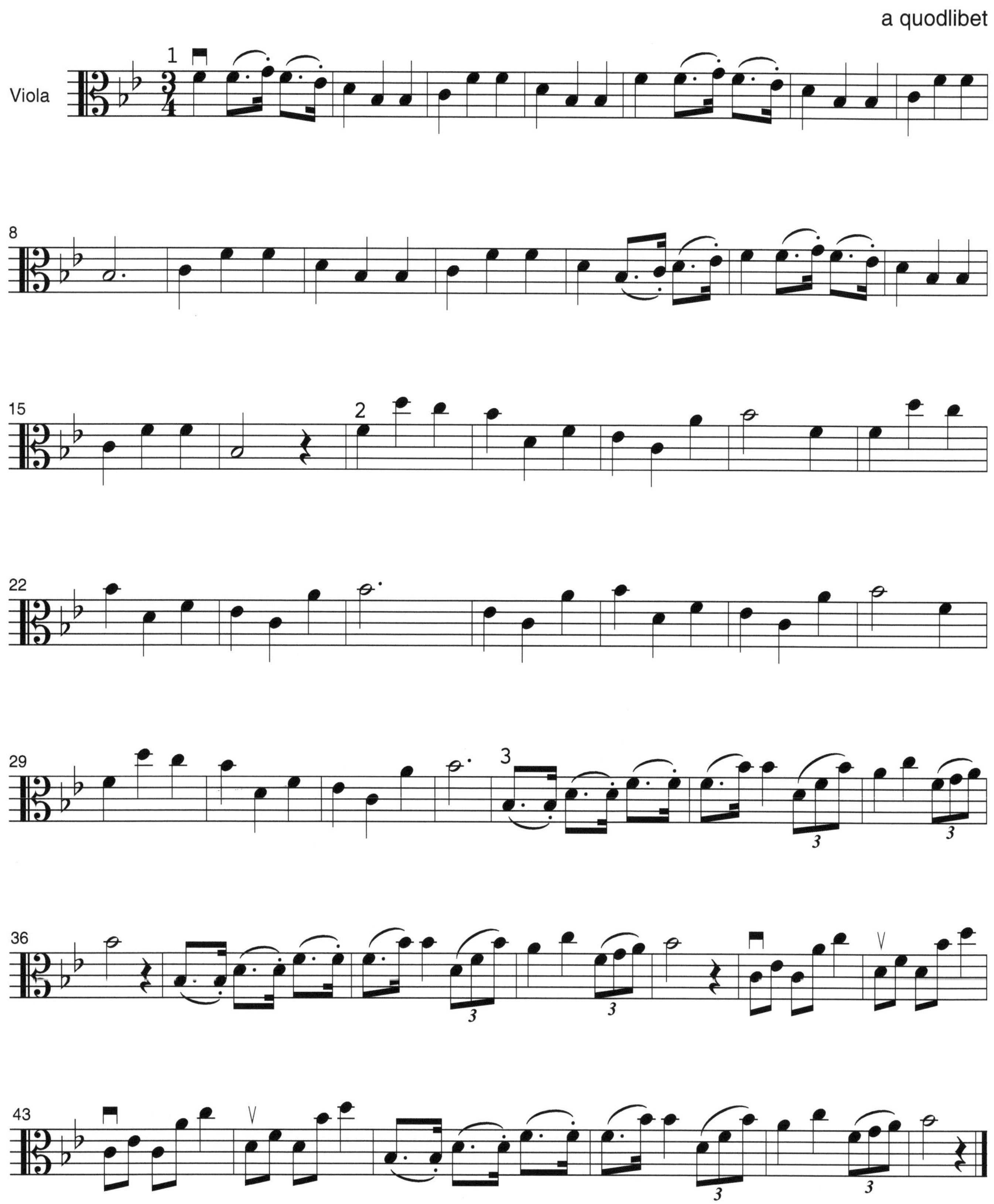

Fair Ursley

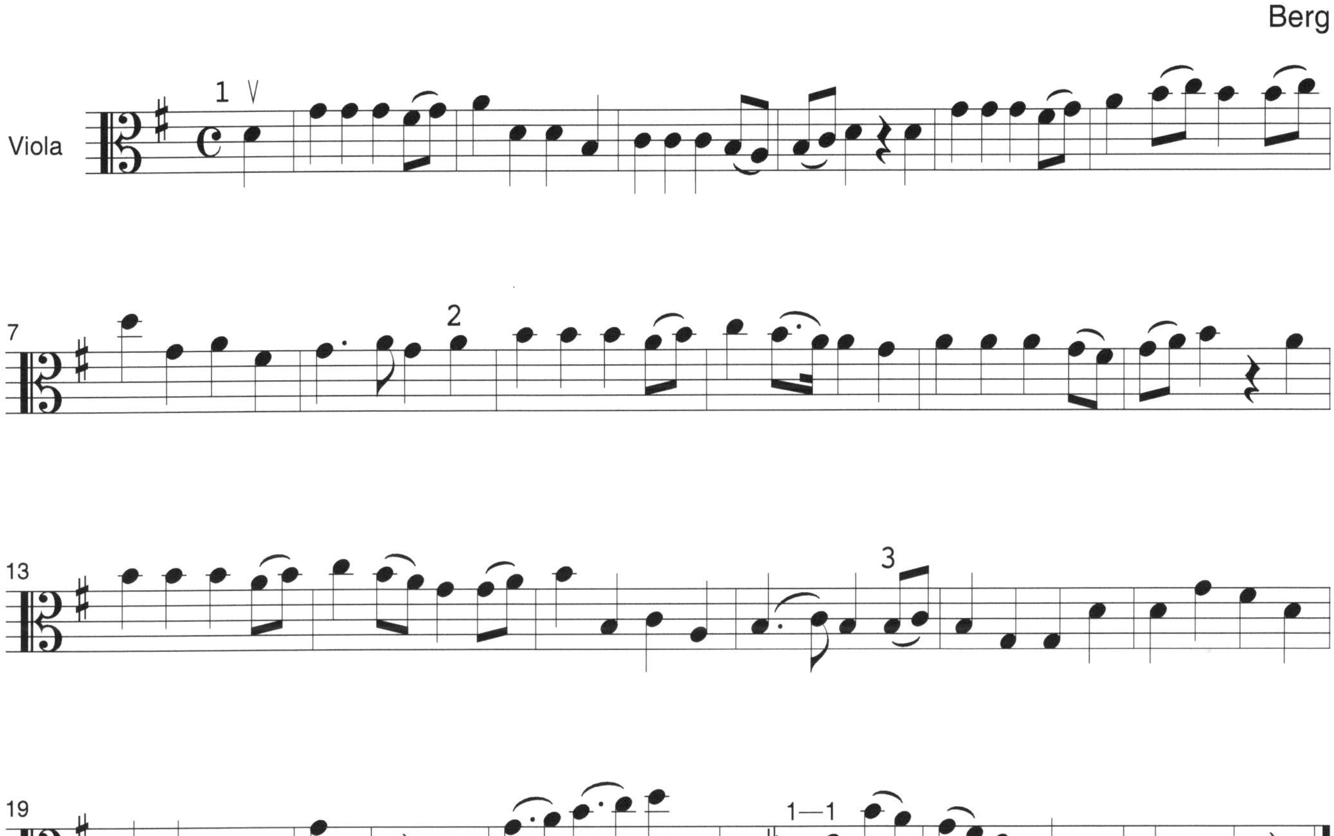

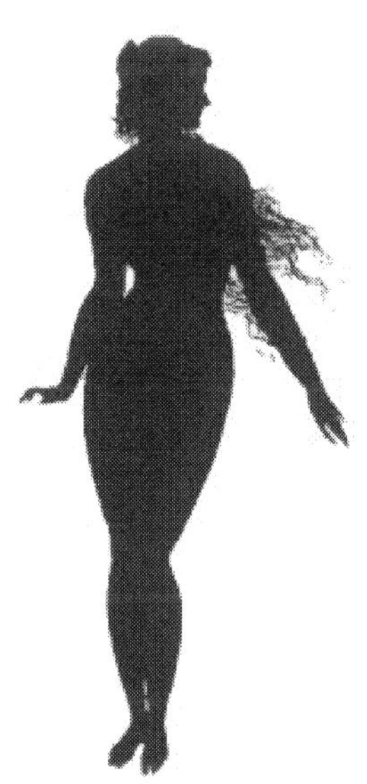

The Hunters

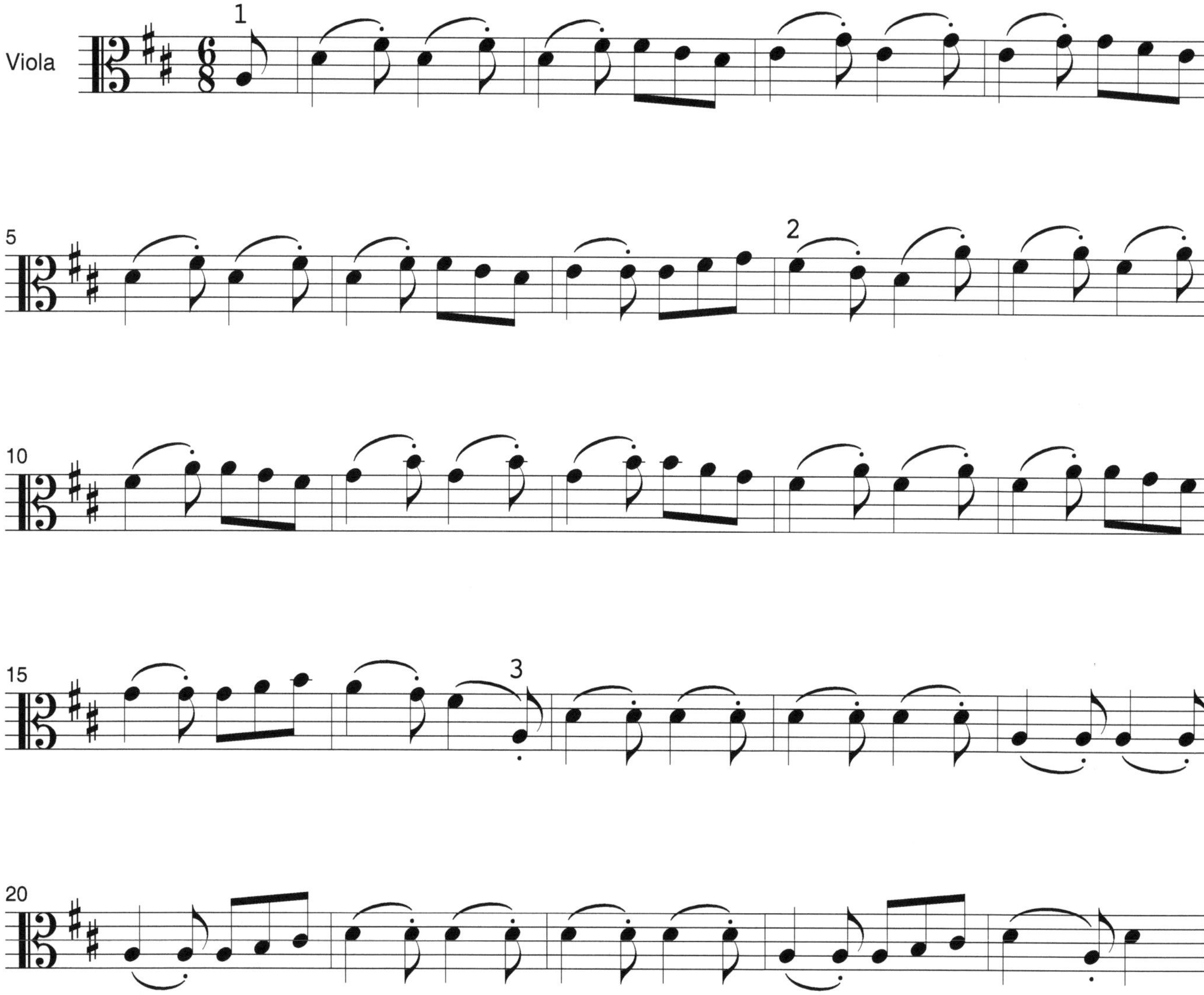

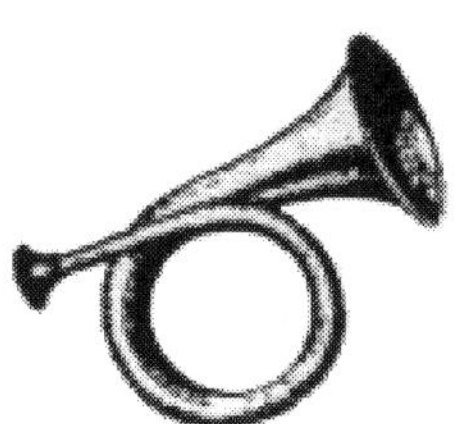

Sumer is Icumen In

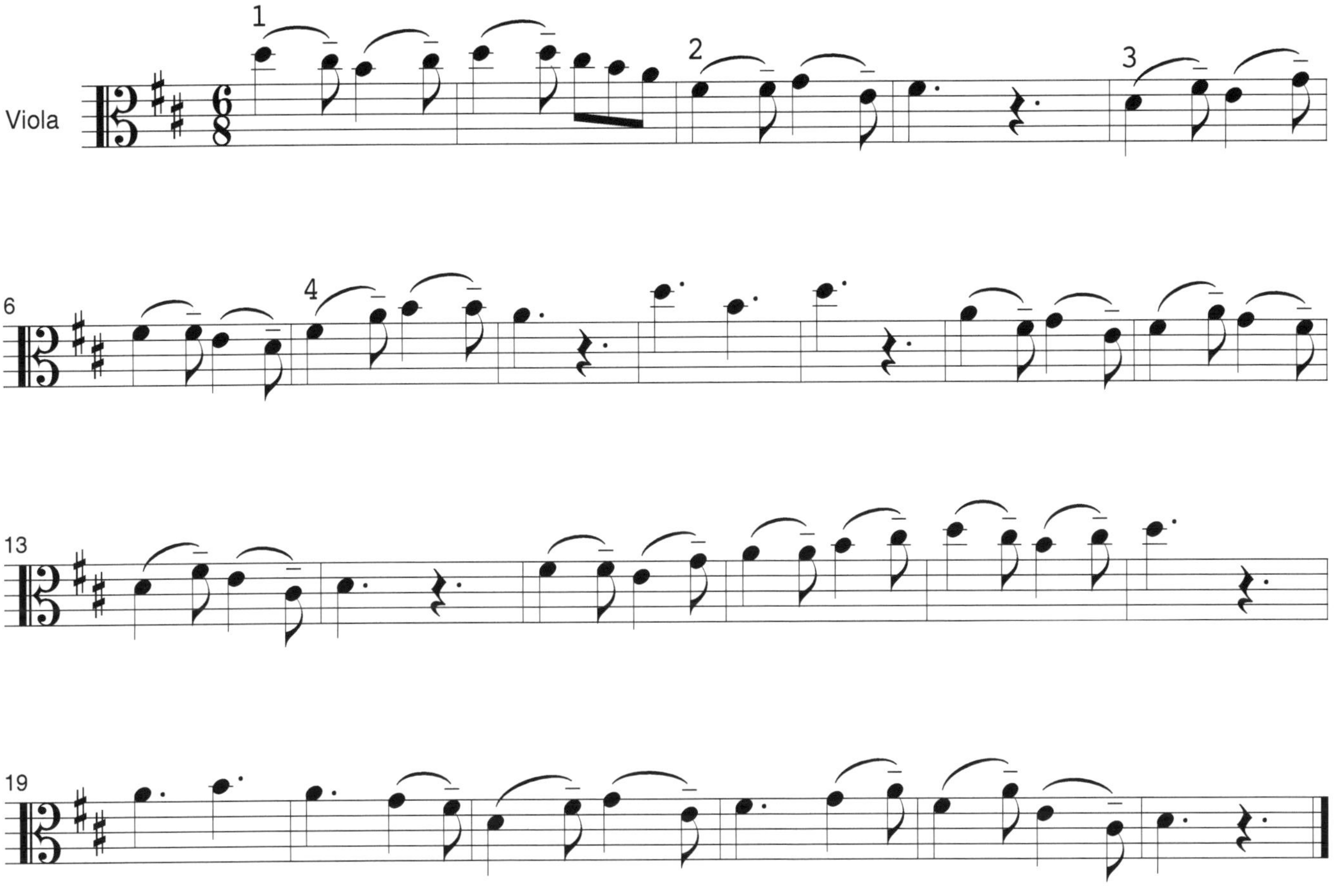

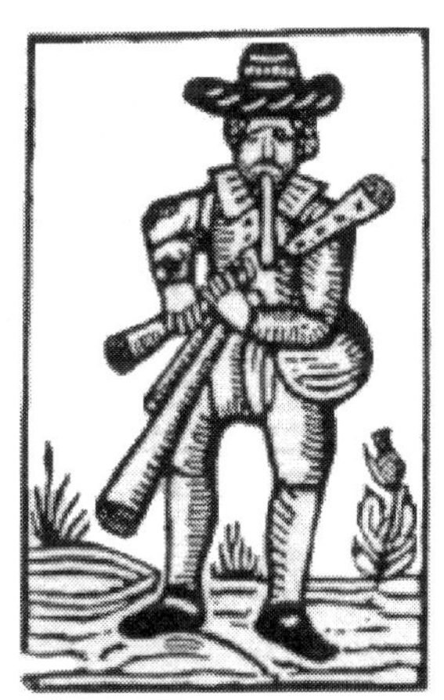

All Who Sing

Goodbar of Canterbury

Viola

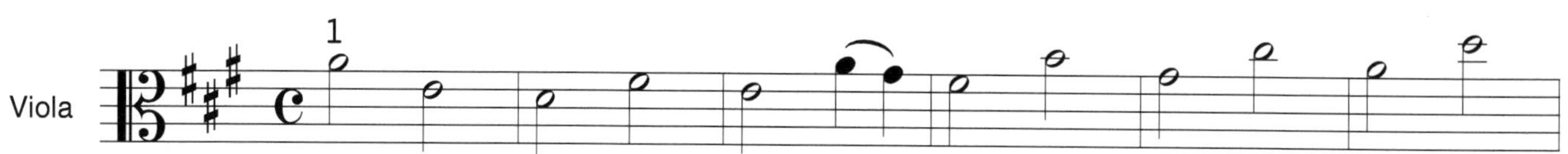

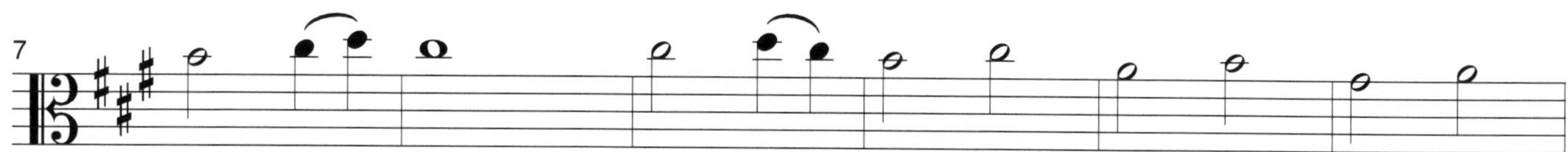

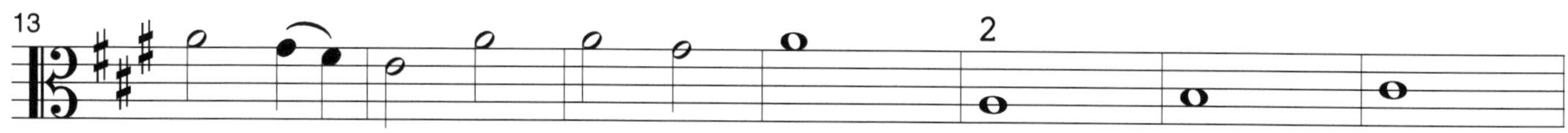

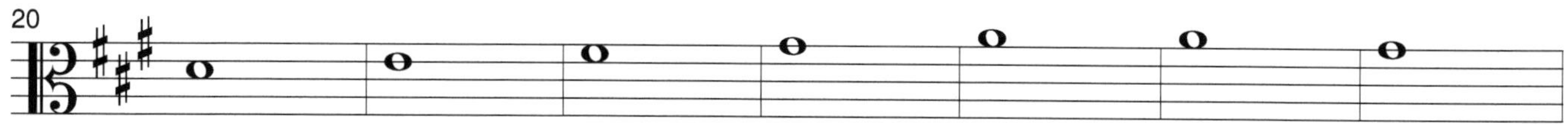

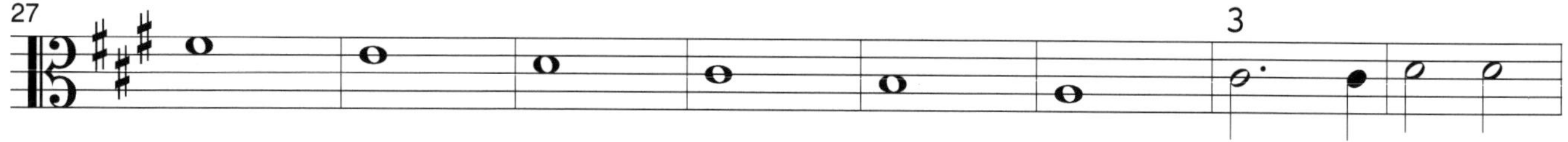

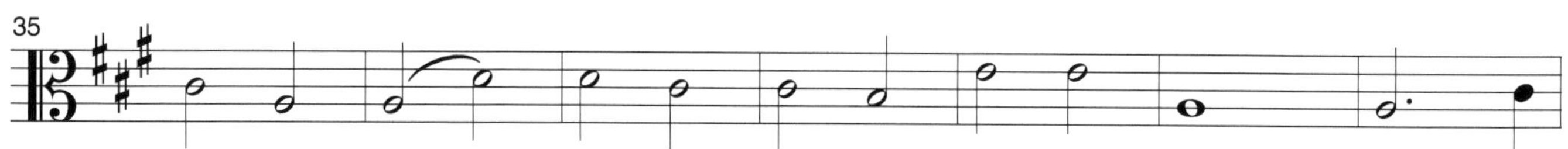

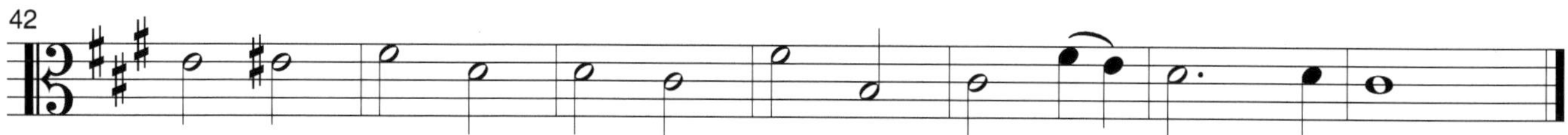

Life Span

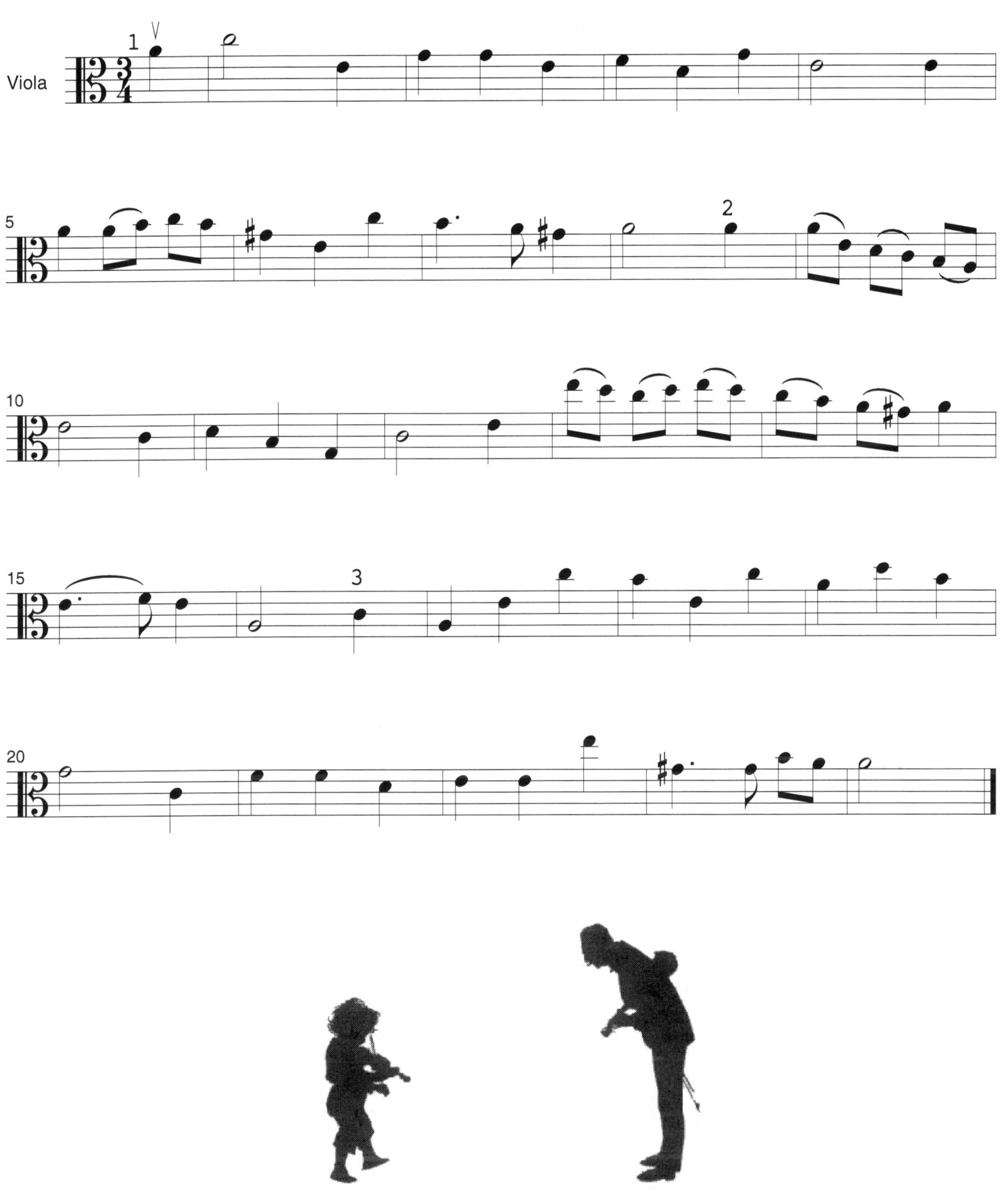

The Street Cries of Oxford Town

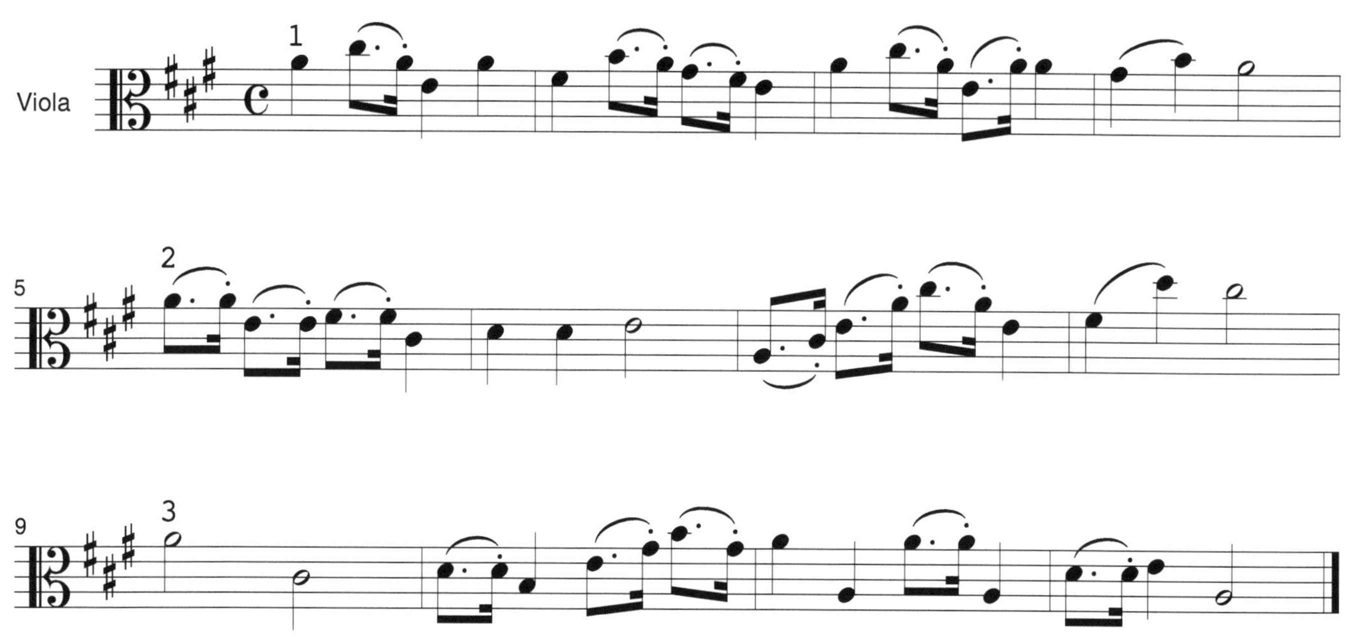

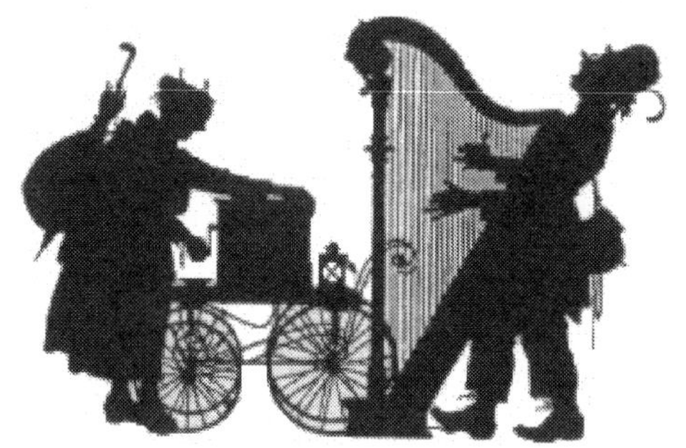

The Oak

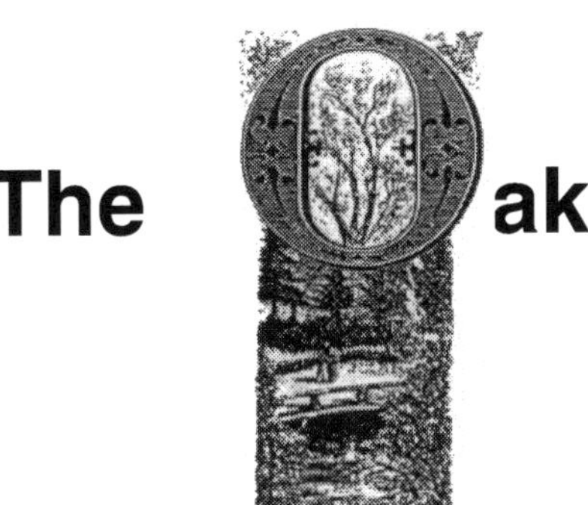

Hayes

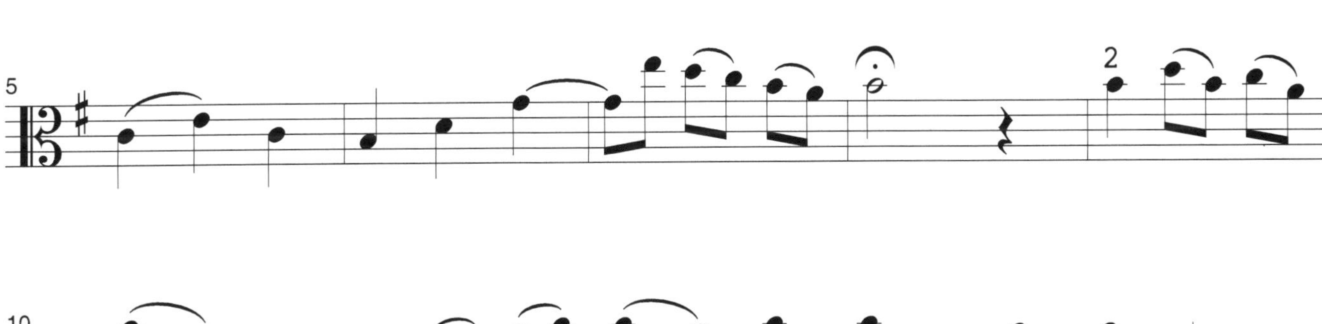
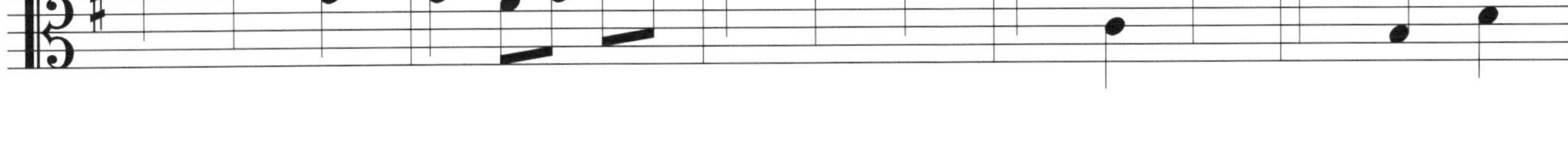
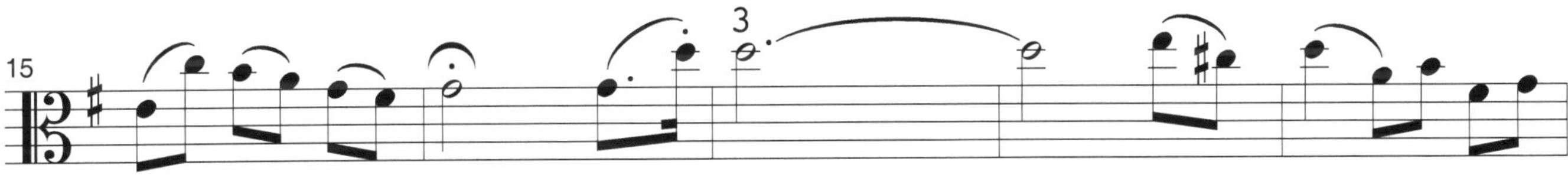
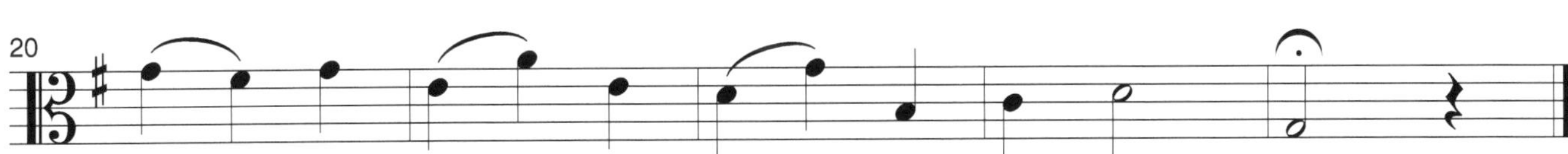

The Sweet Pleasures of Spring

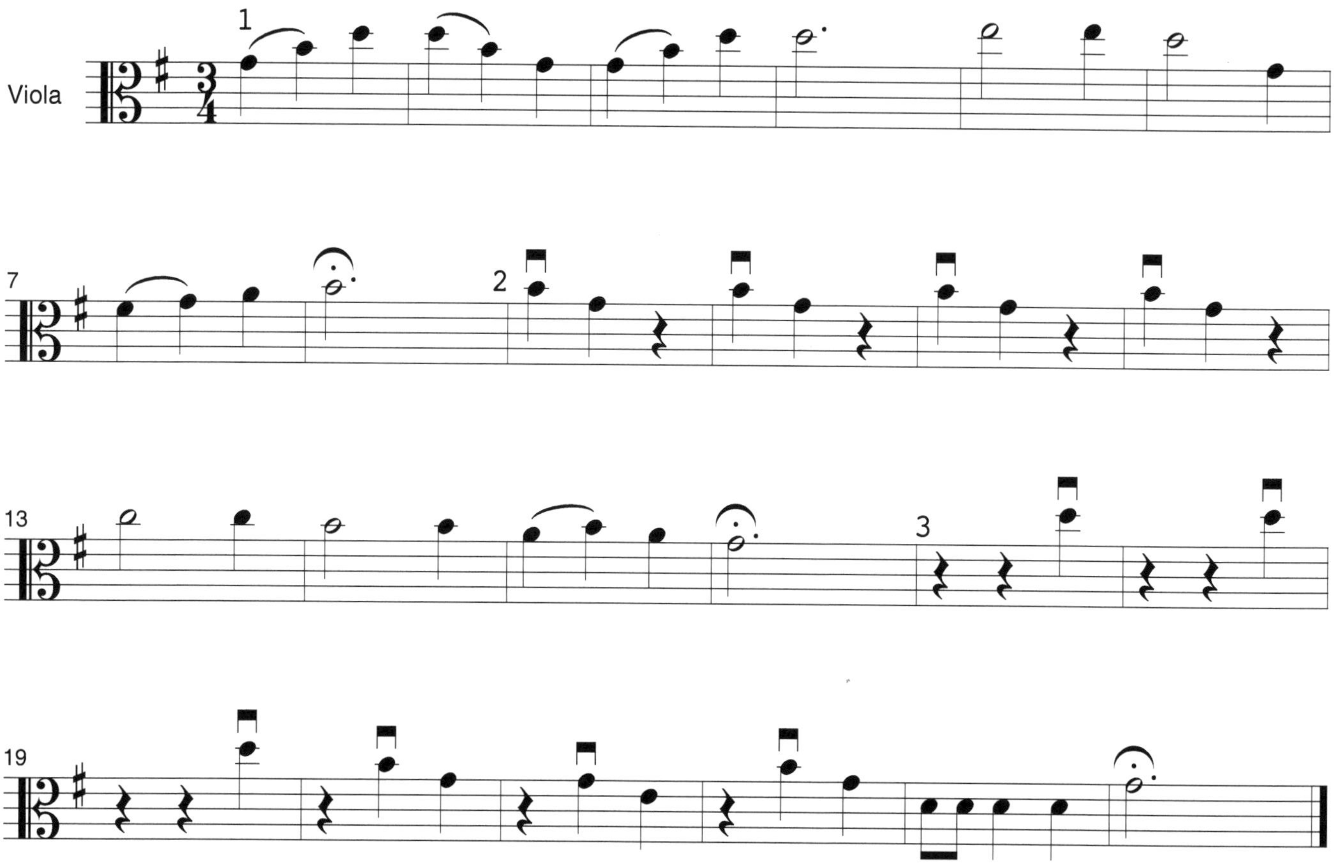

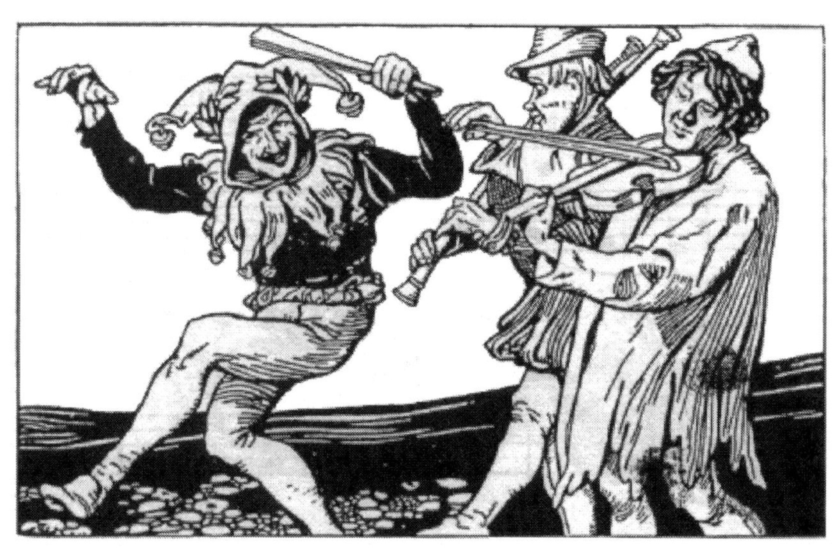

Beethoven's Round

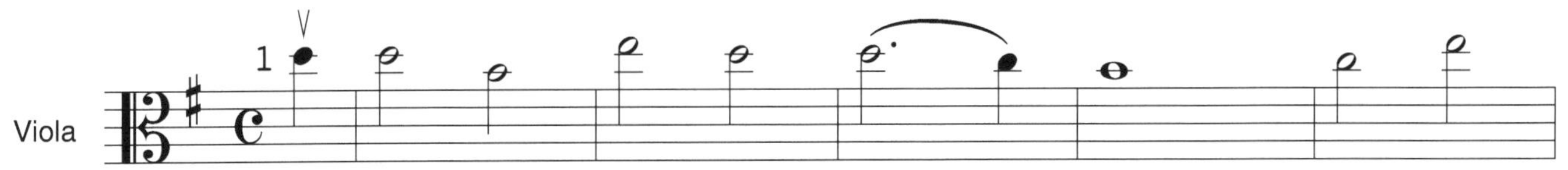

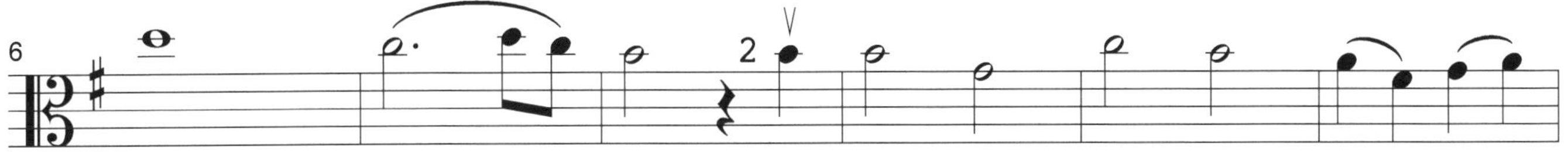

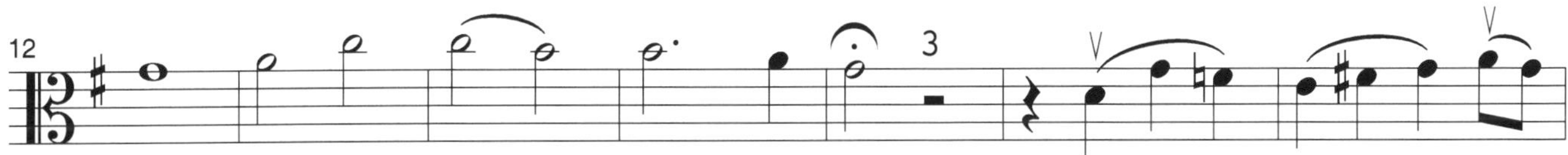

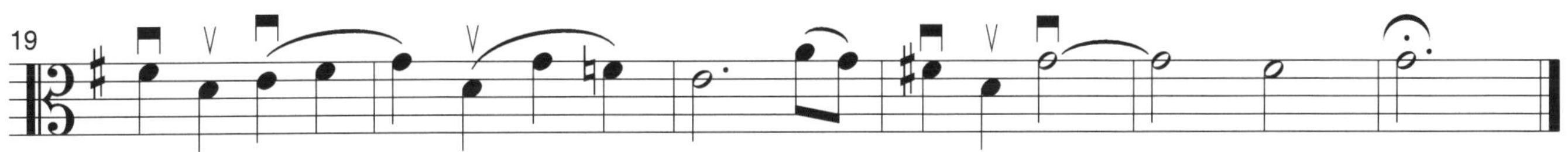

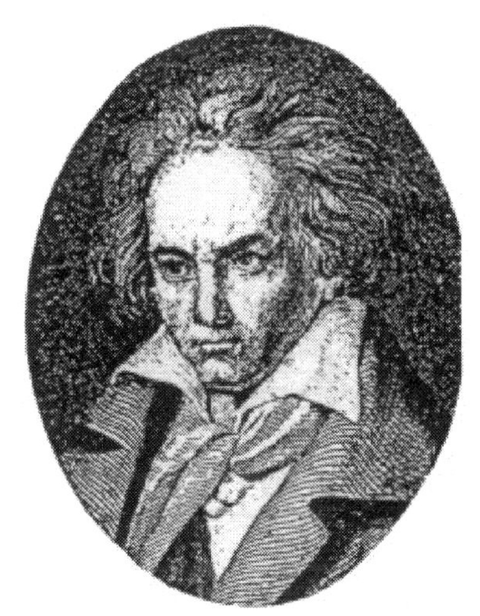

SENIOR LEVEL REPERTOIRE

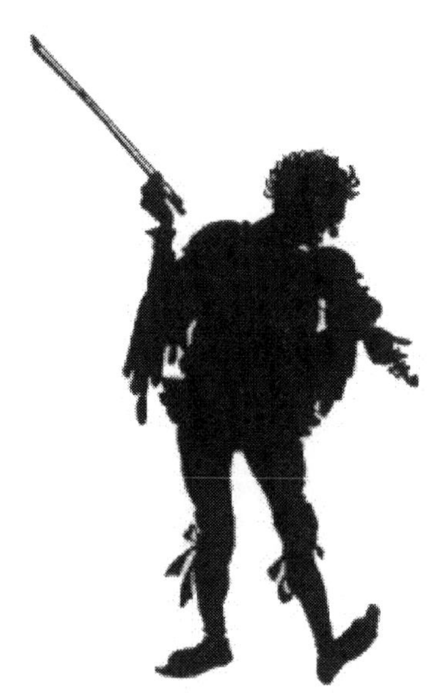

OLD NOTES—WITH A NEW NAME

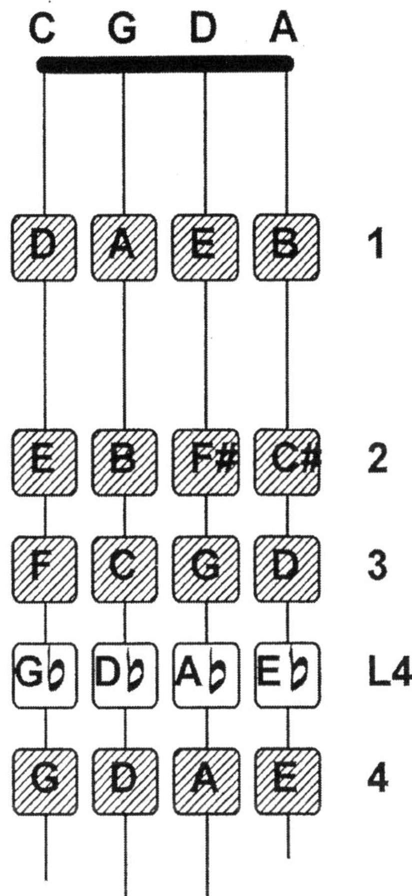

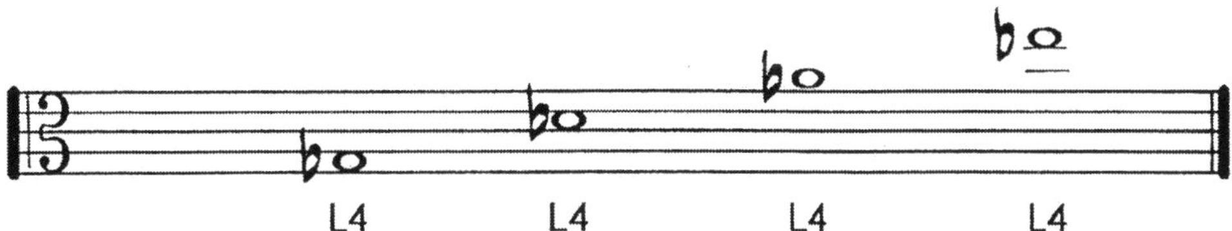

Barcarolle

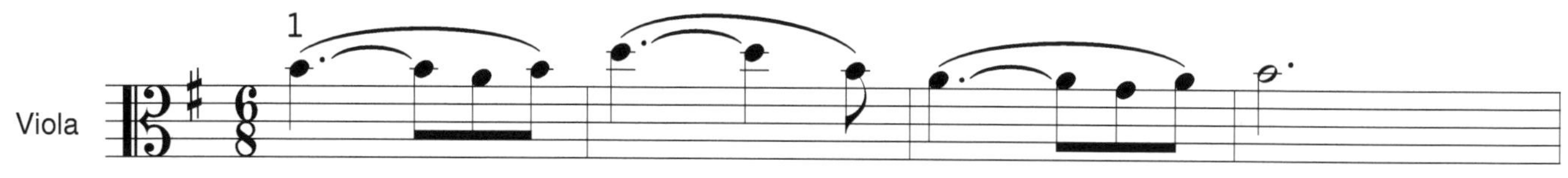

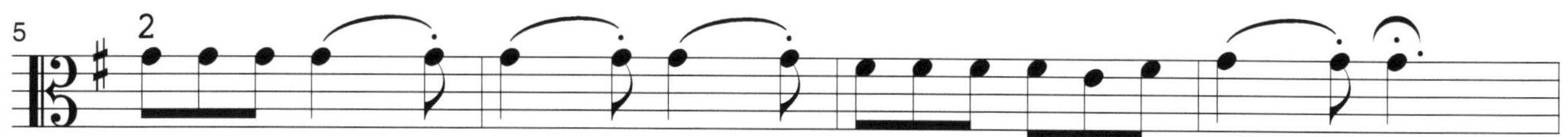

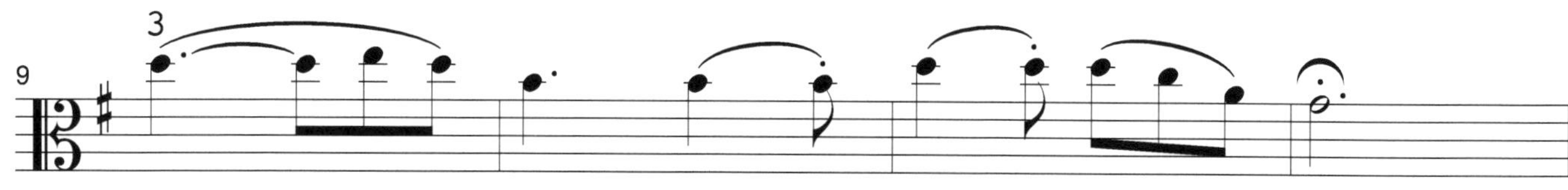

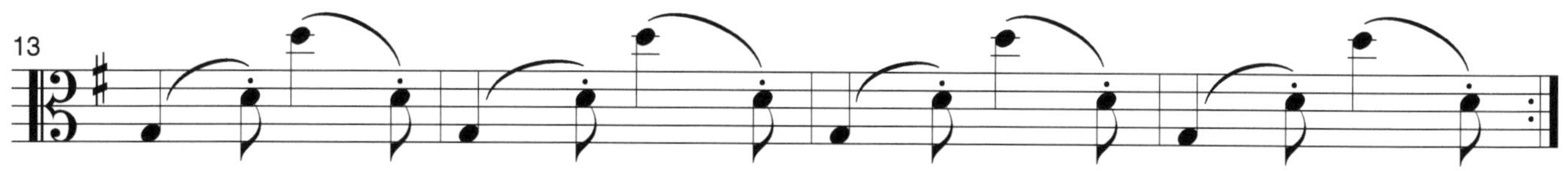

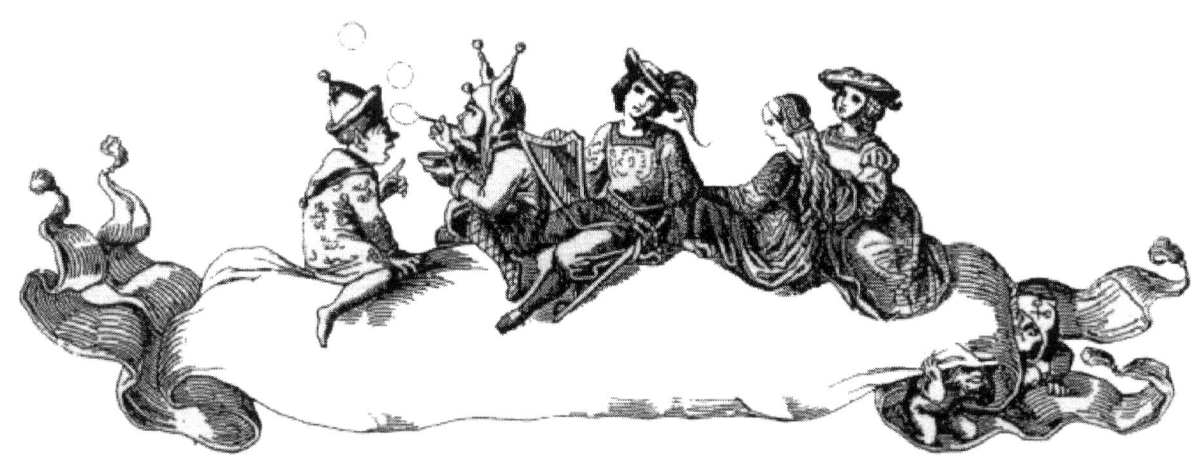

Pratty Naun, a Scottish Catch

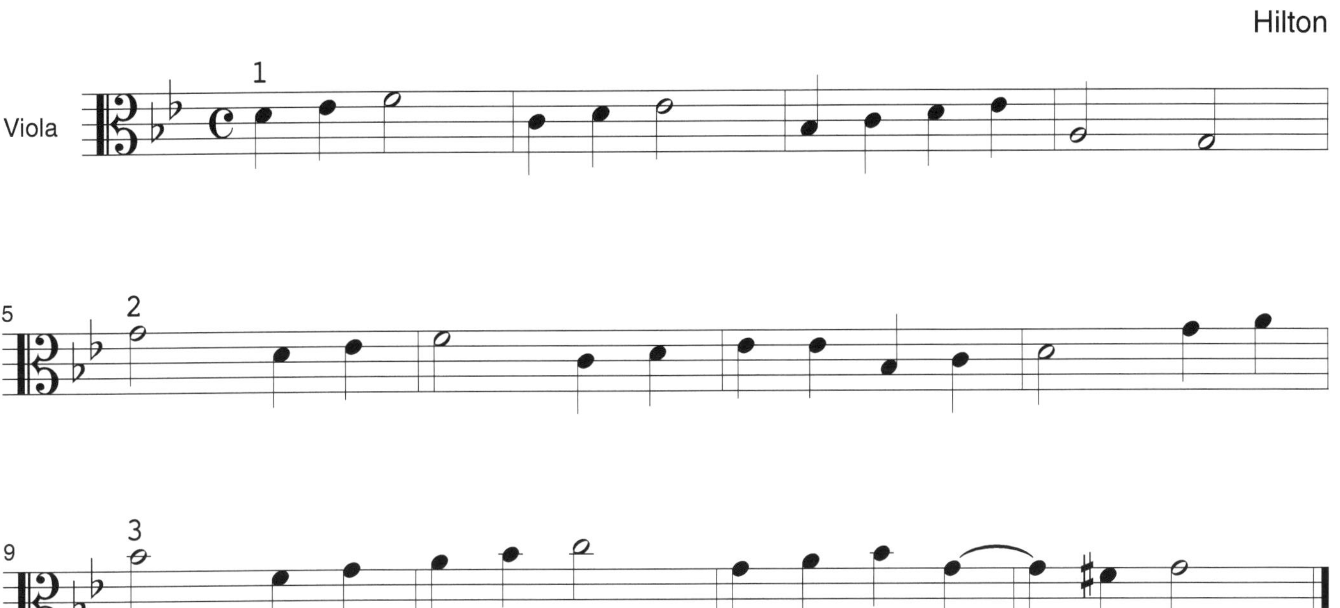

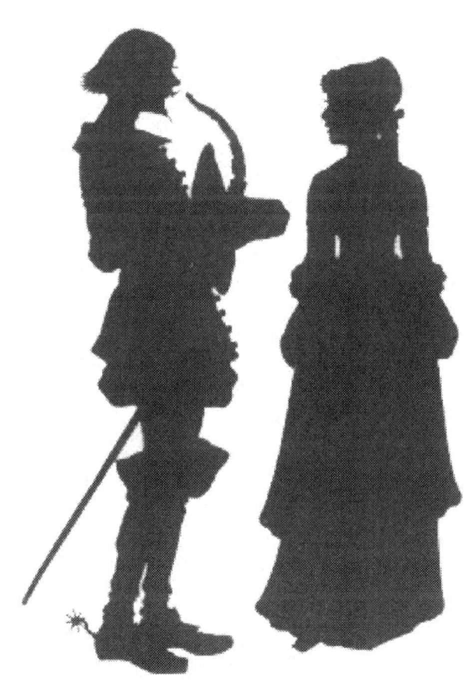

Sing and Be Merry

Berg

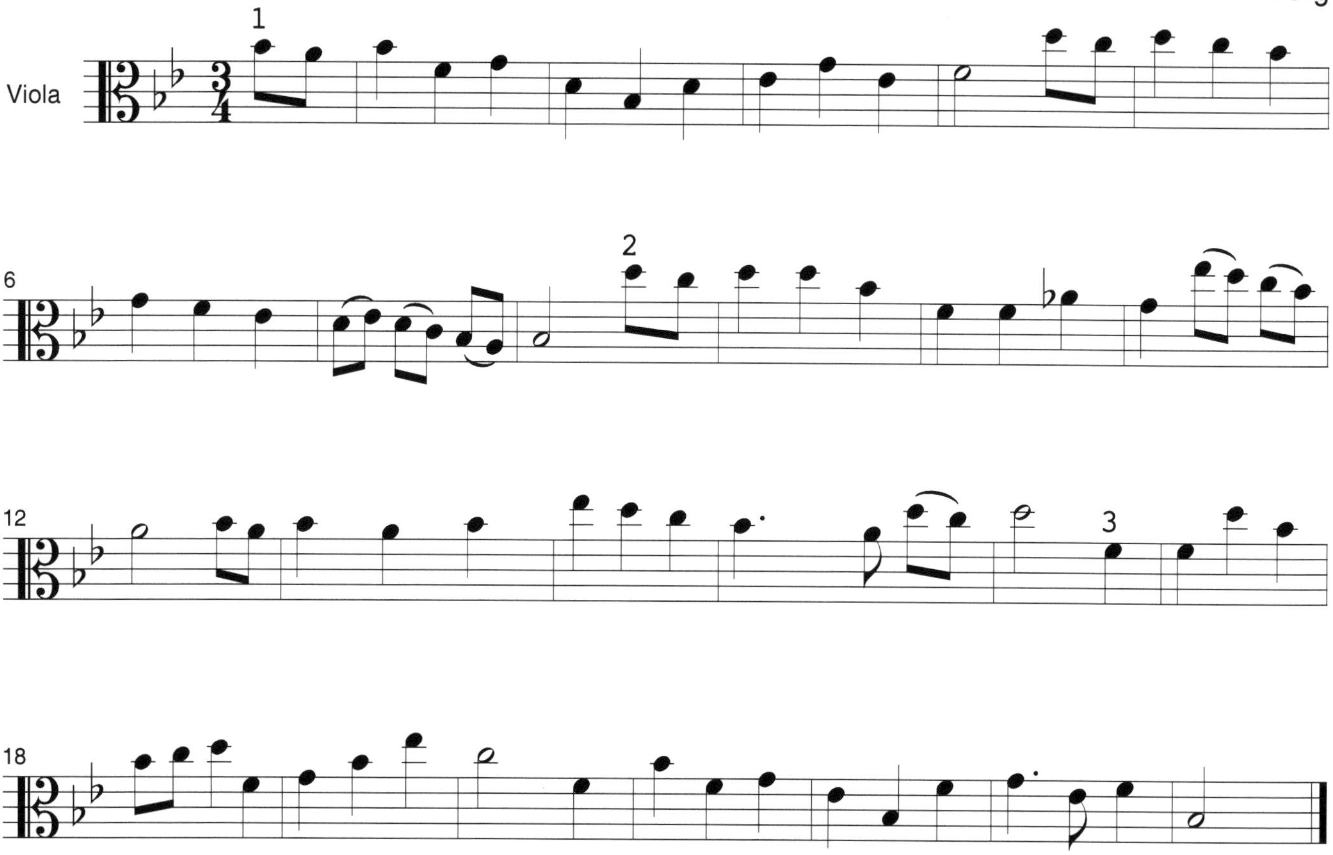

Viola

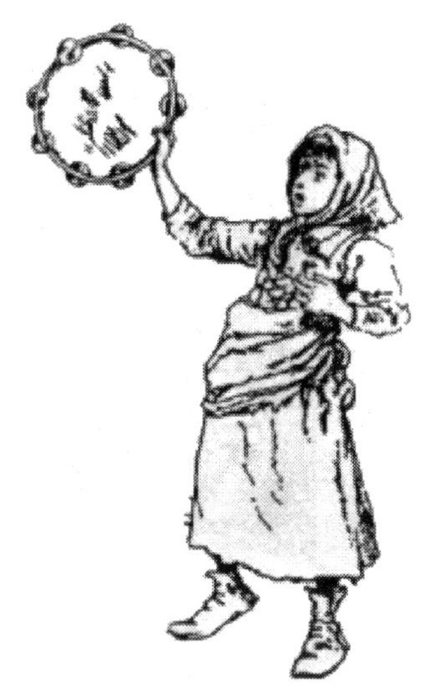

Sing We This Roundelay

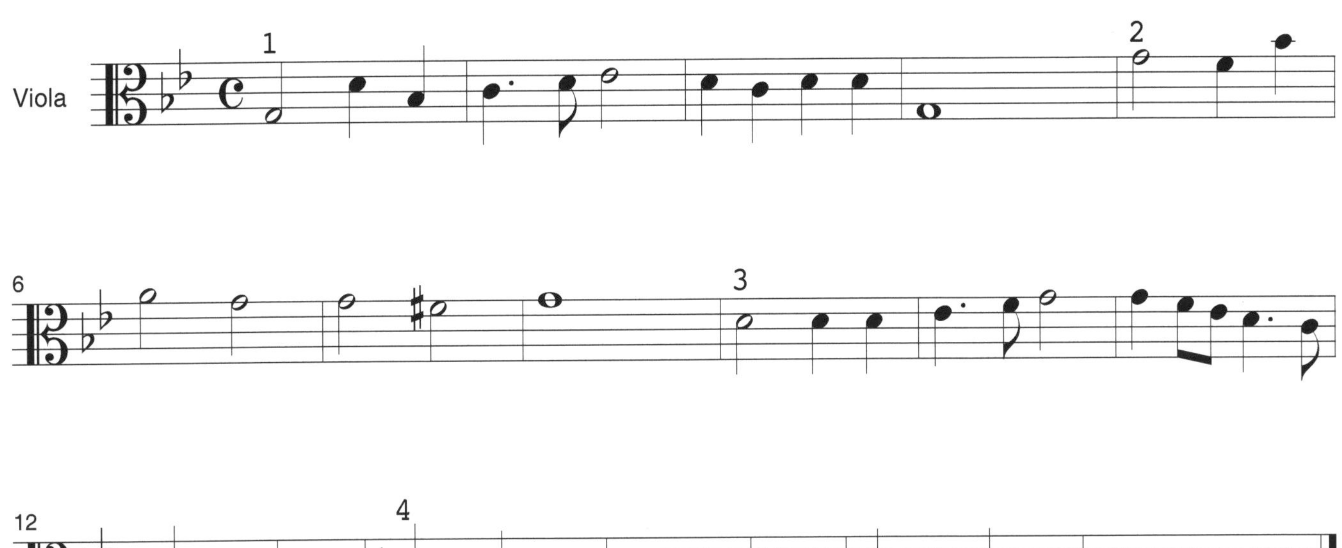

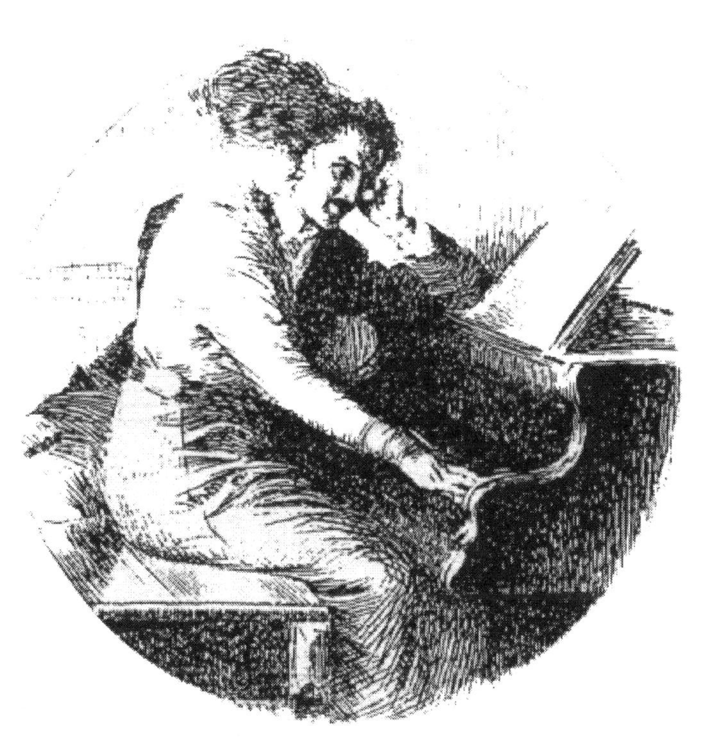

Ave Maria

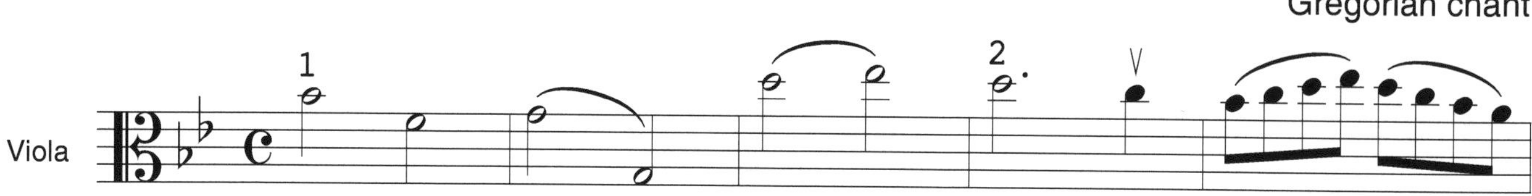

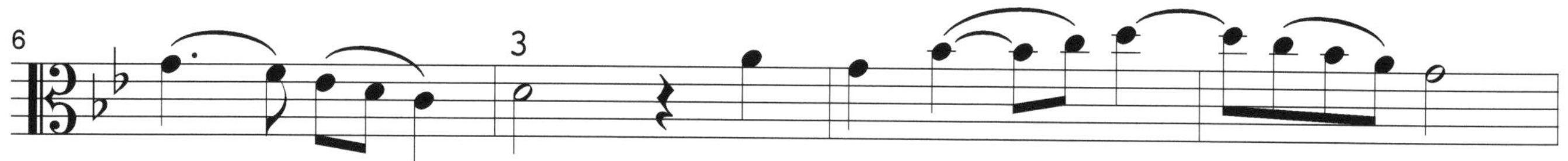

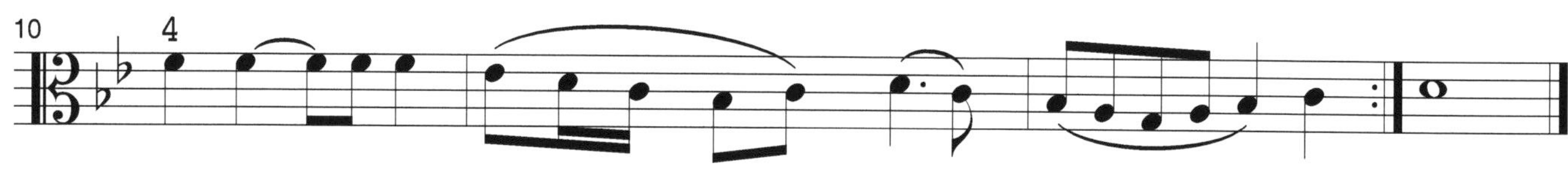

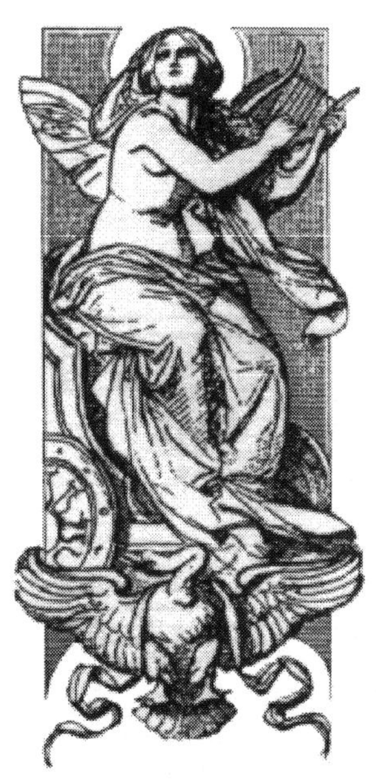

Bononcini's Spring

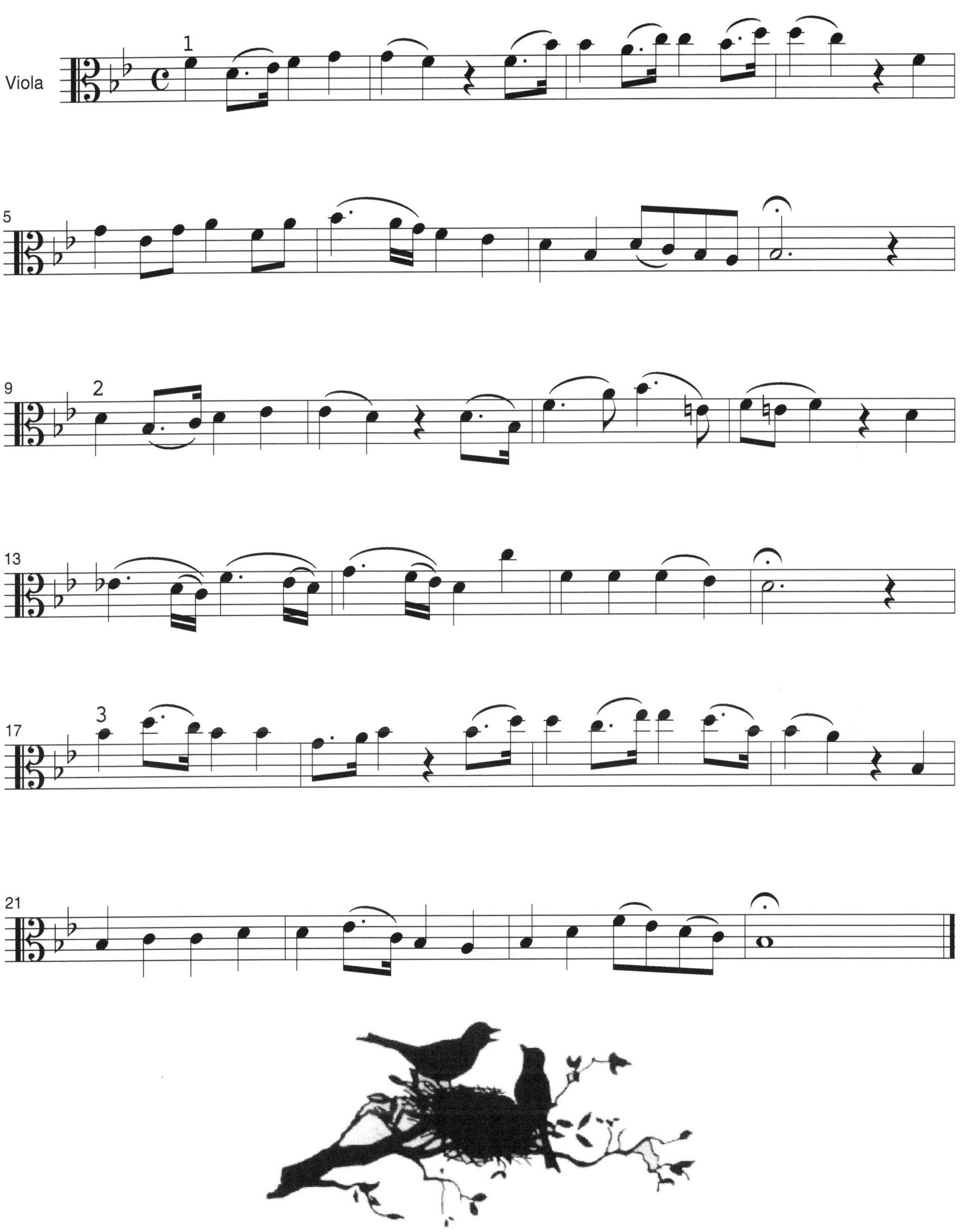

Gabrial John

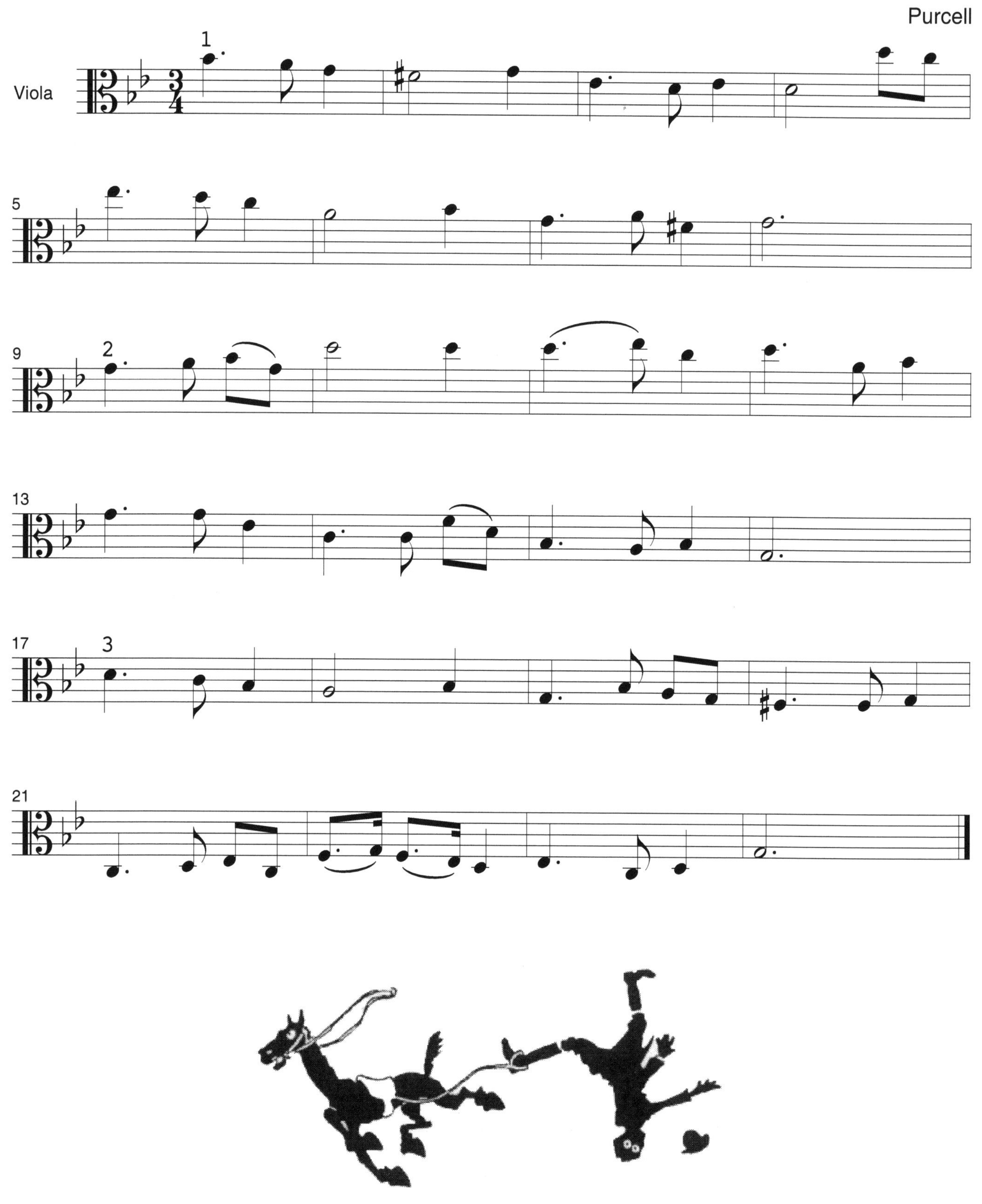

Callcott's Round

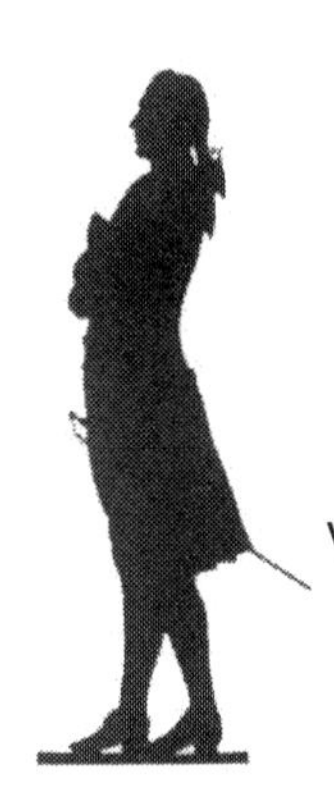

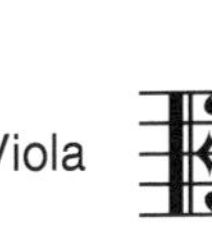

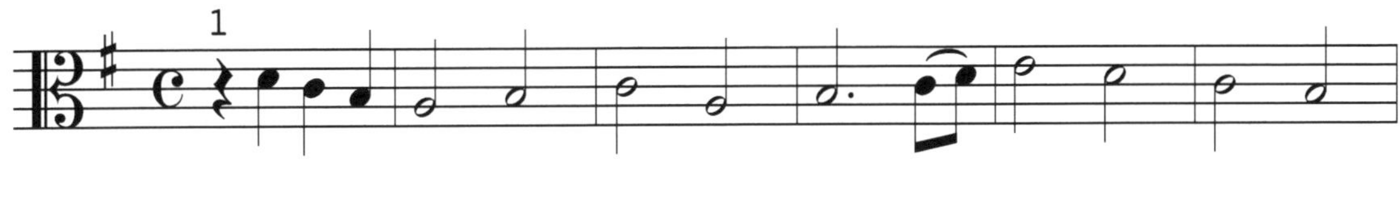

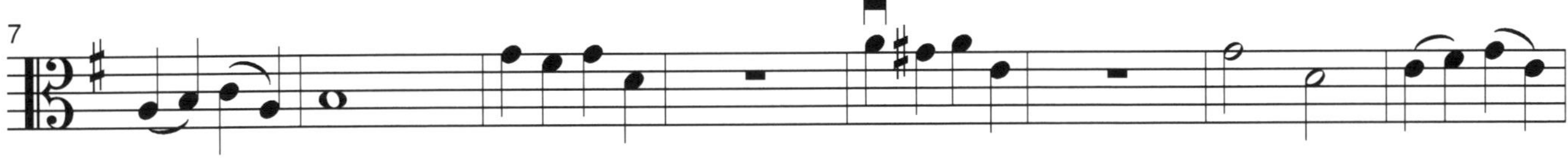

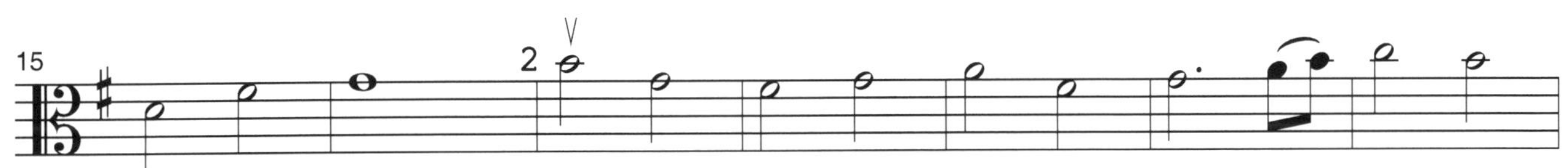

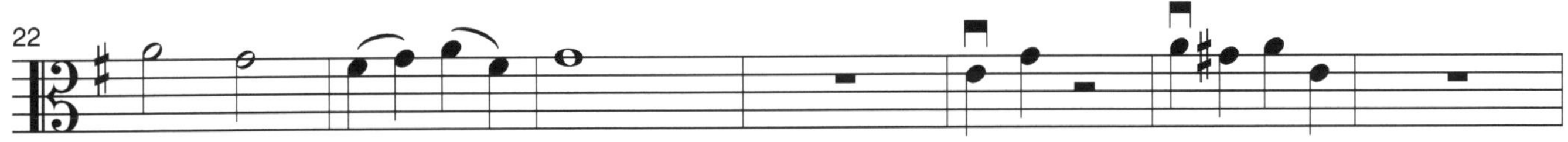

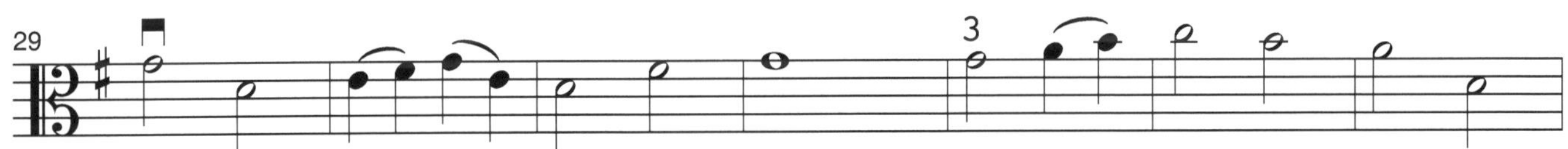

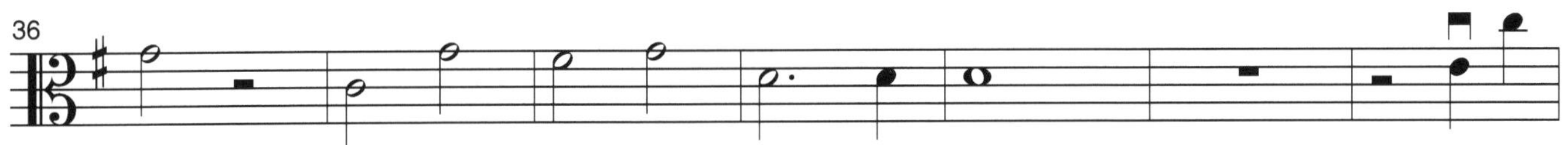

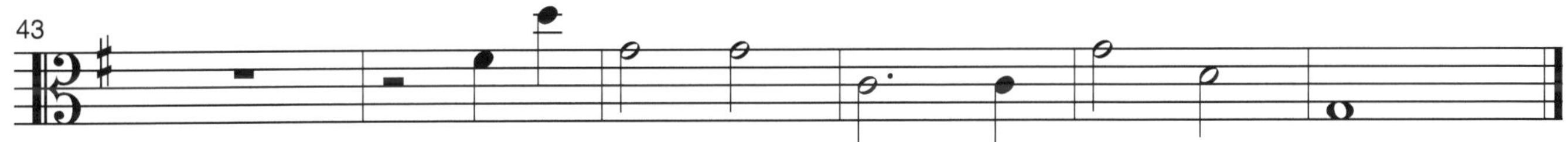

Now We Are Met

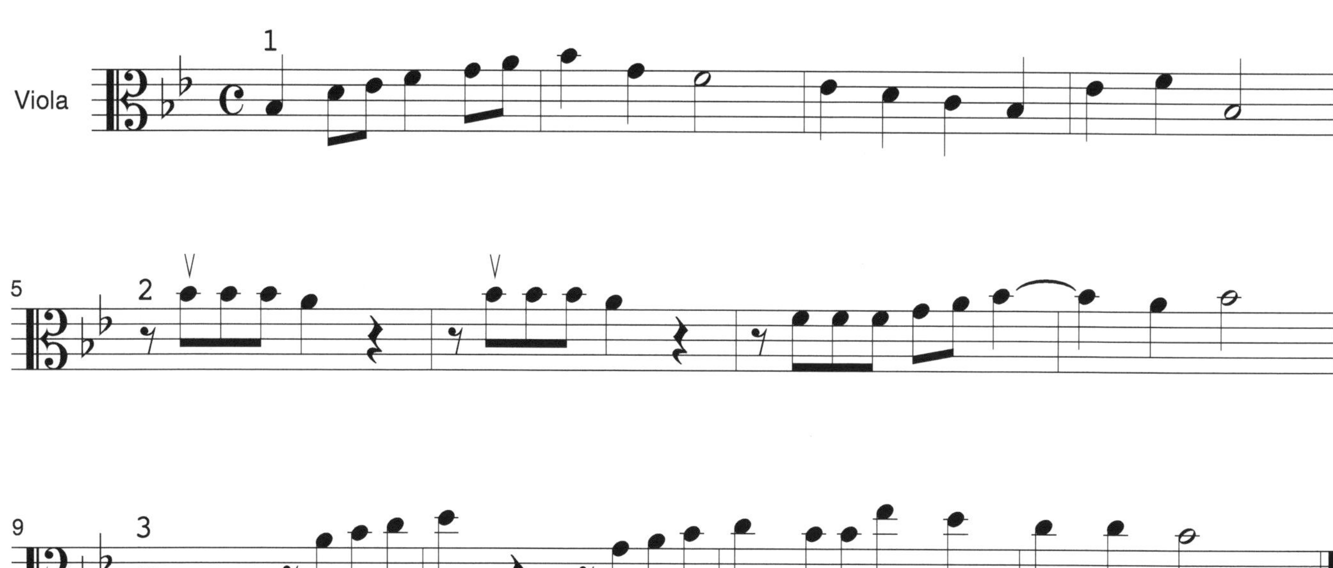

Come Hither

Hilton

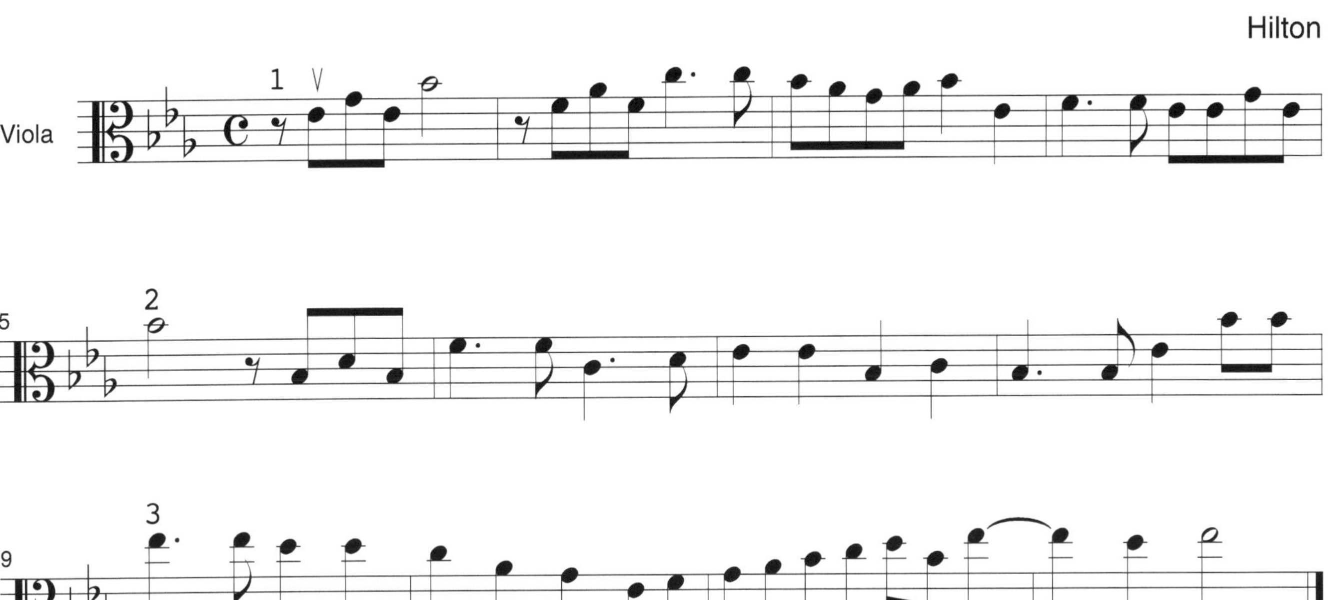

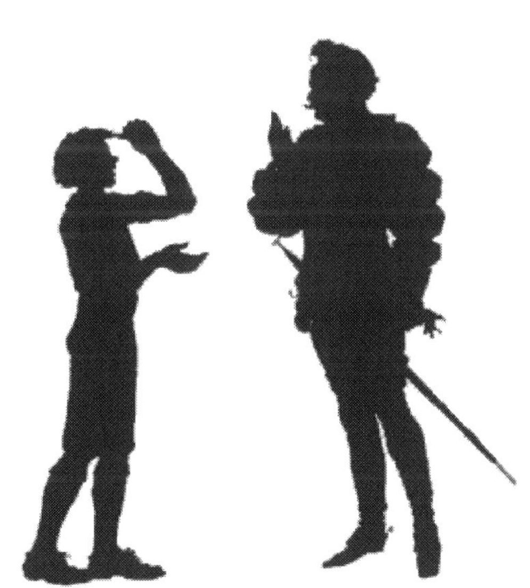

This Hour, My Bonny Lads

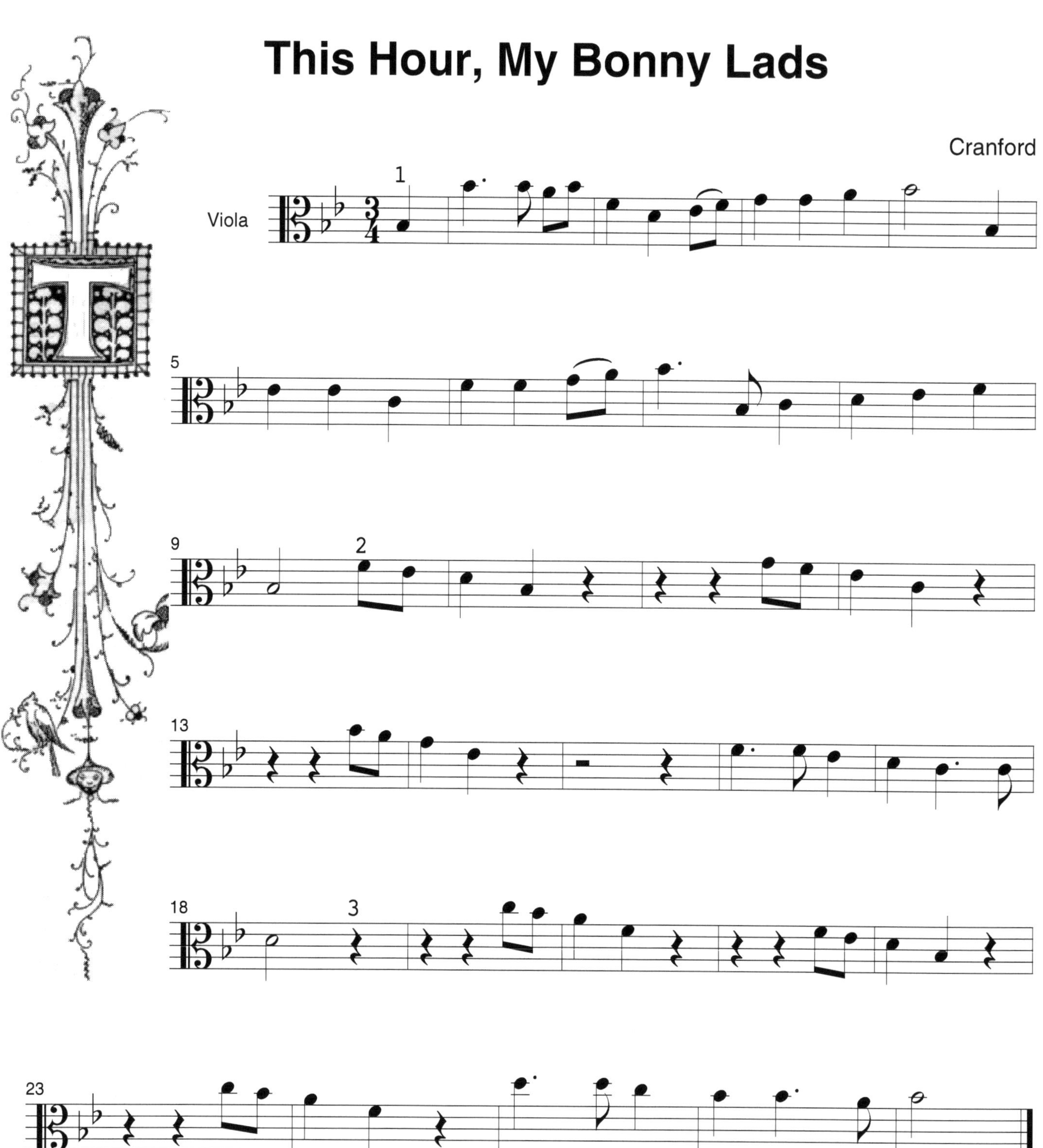

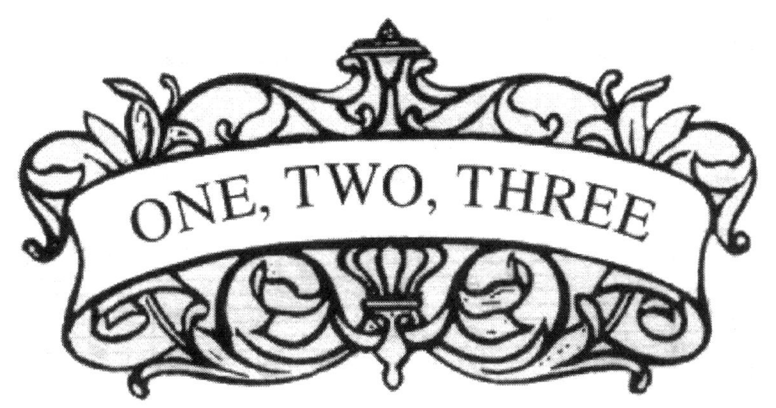

Purcell

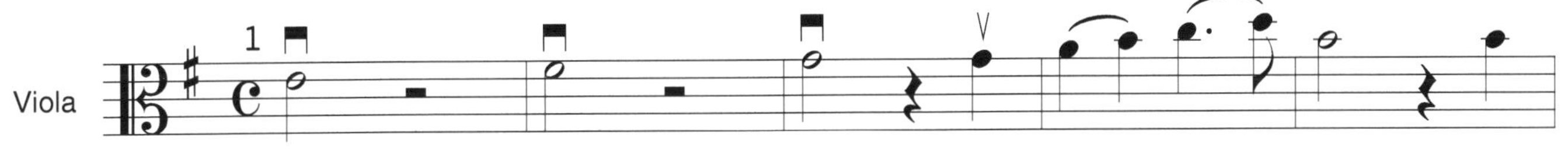

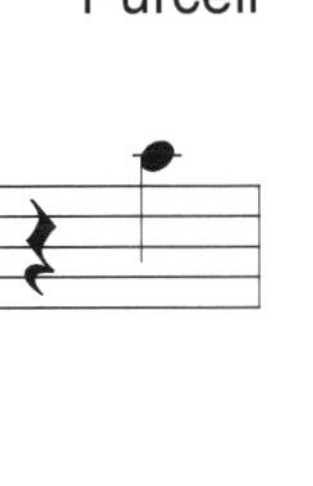

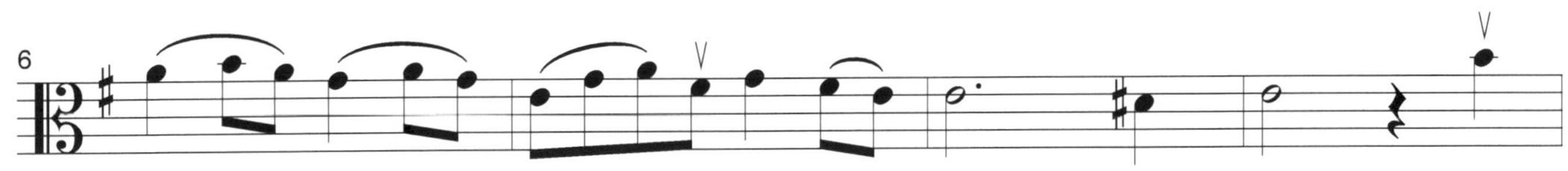

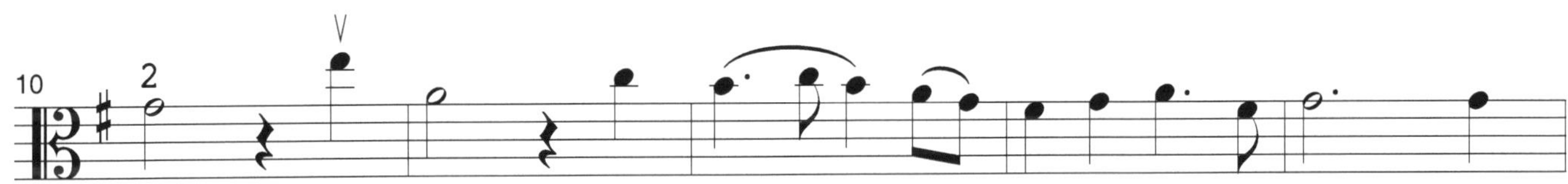

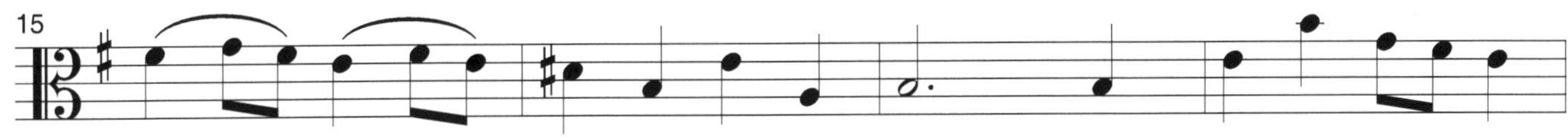

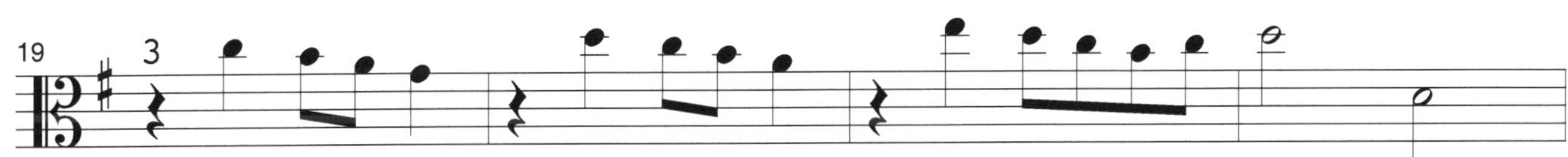

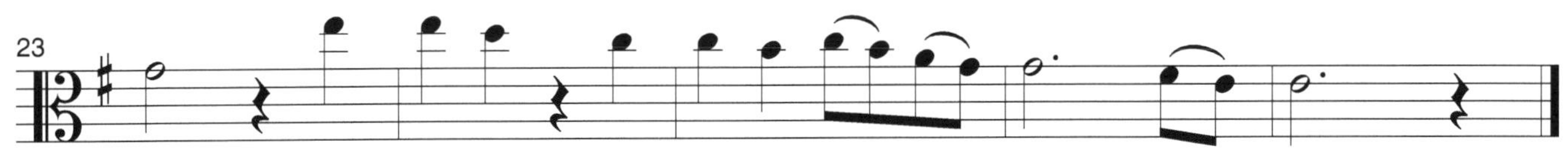

Tread Soft My Friend

Danby

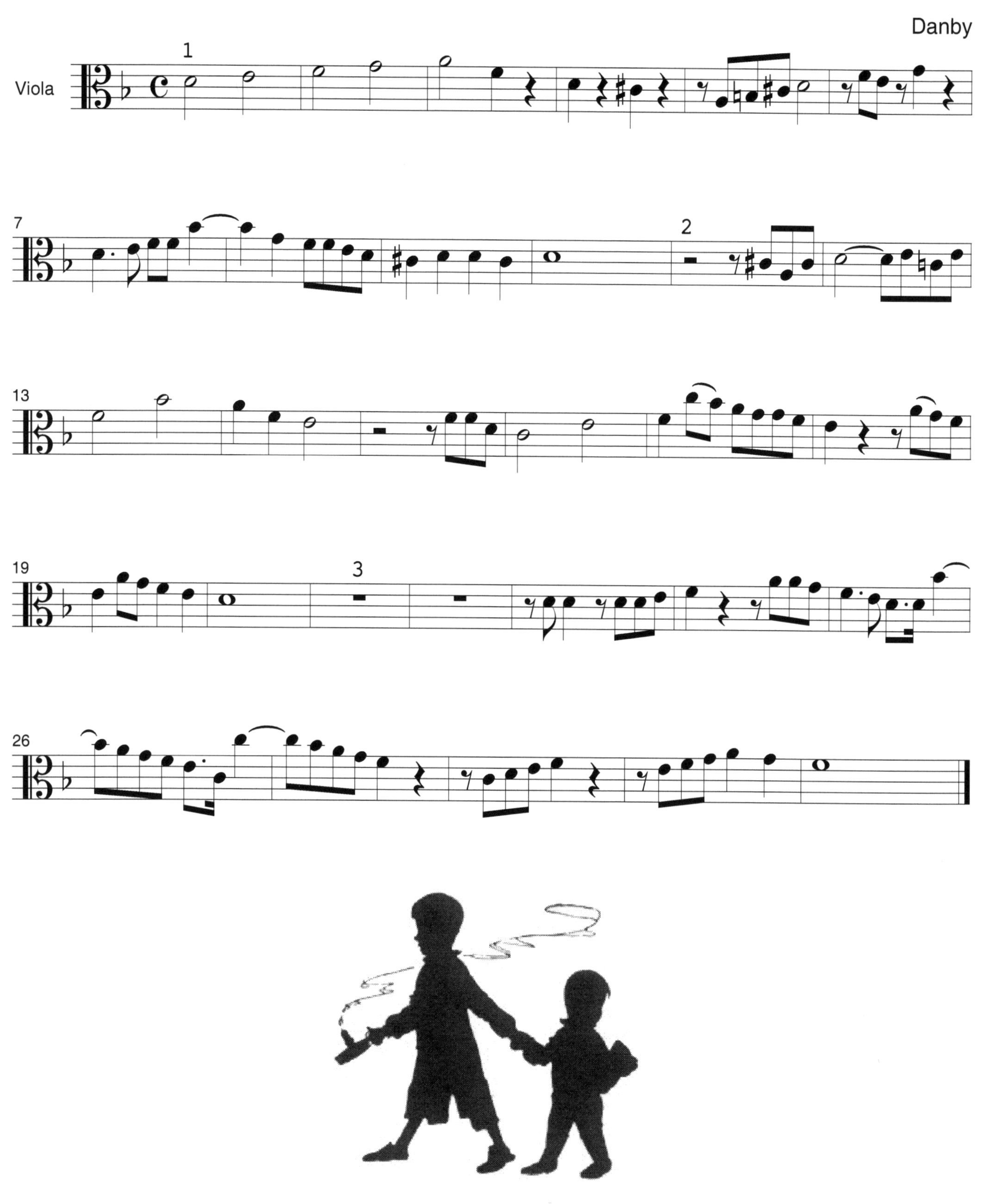

Retreat

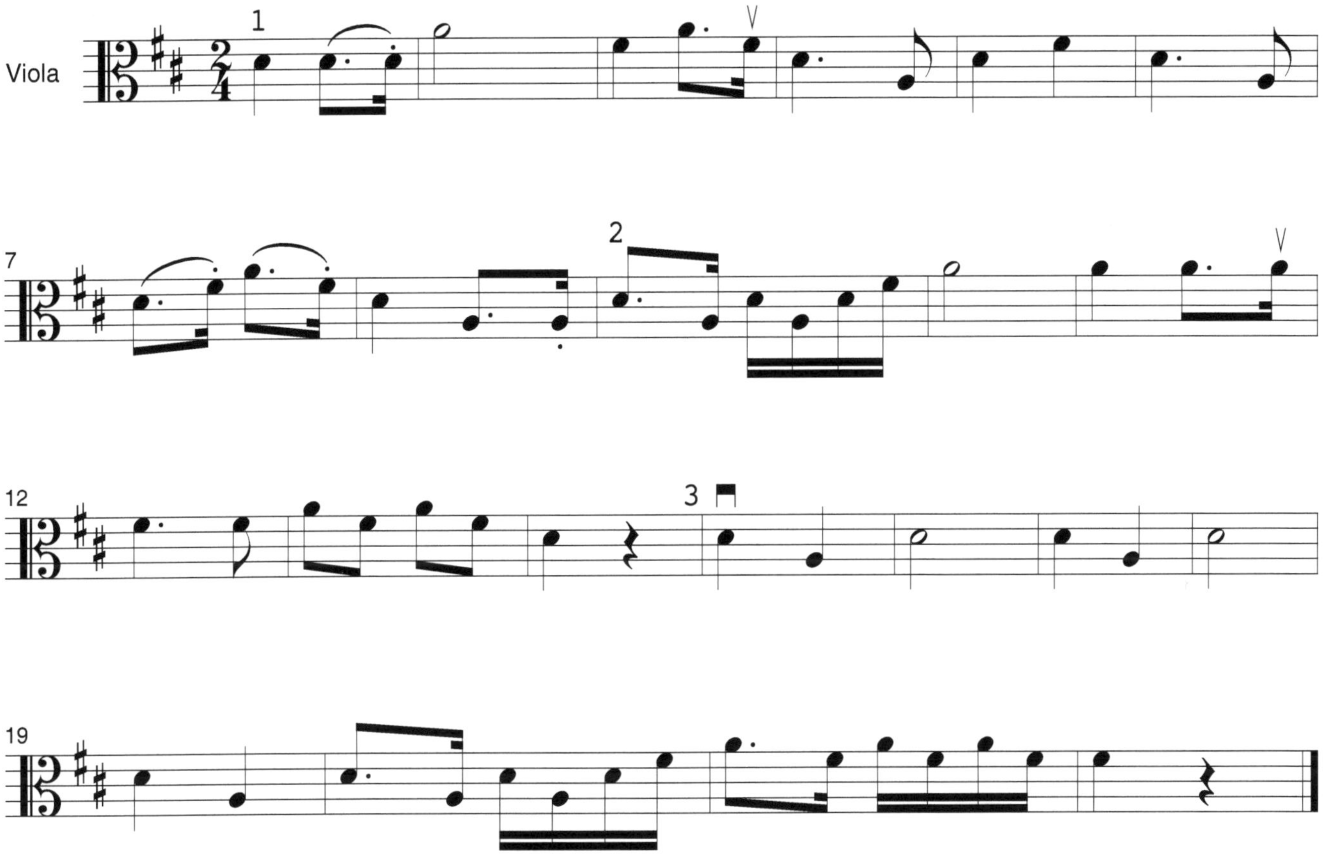

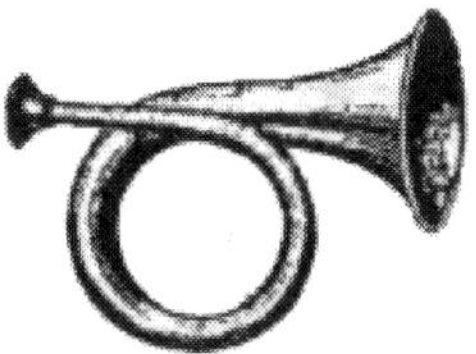

To the Colors

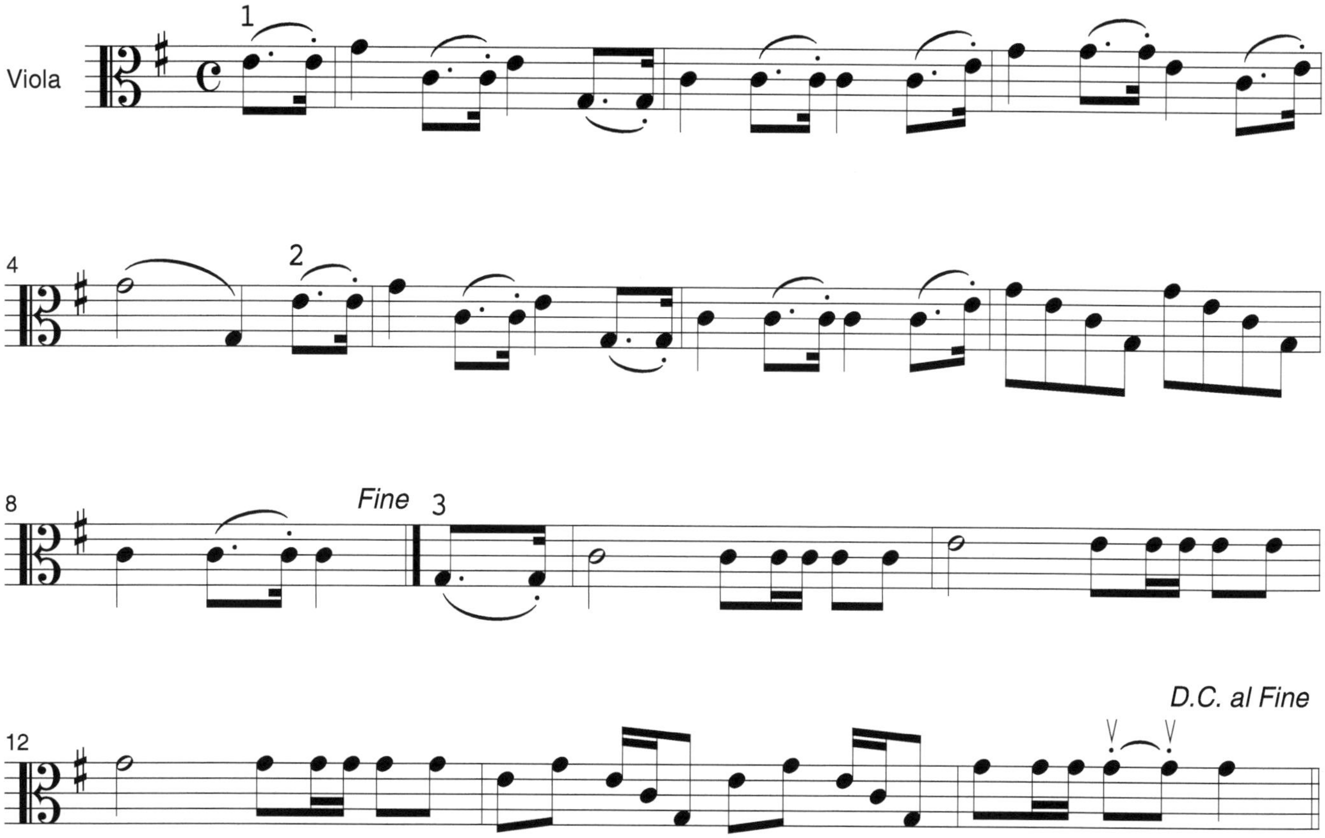

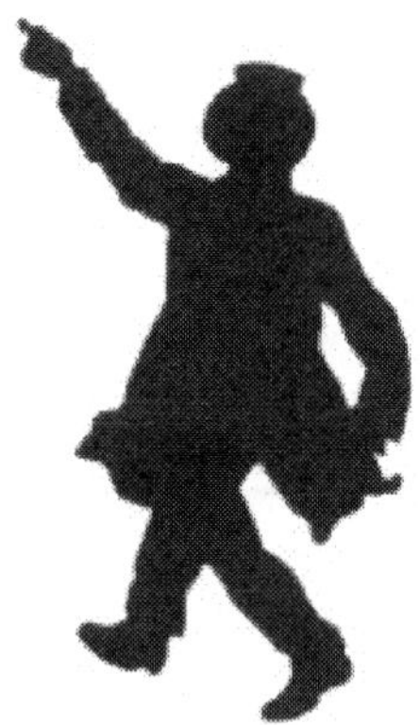

Haida, Haida

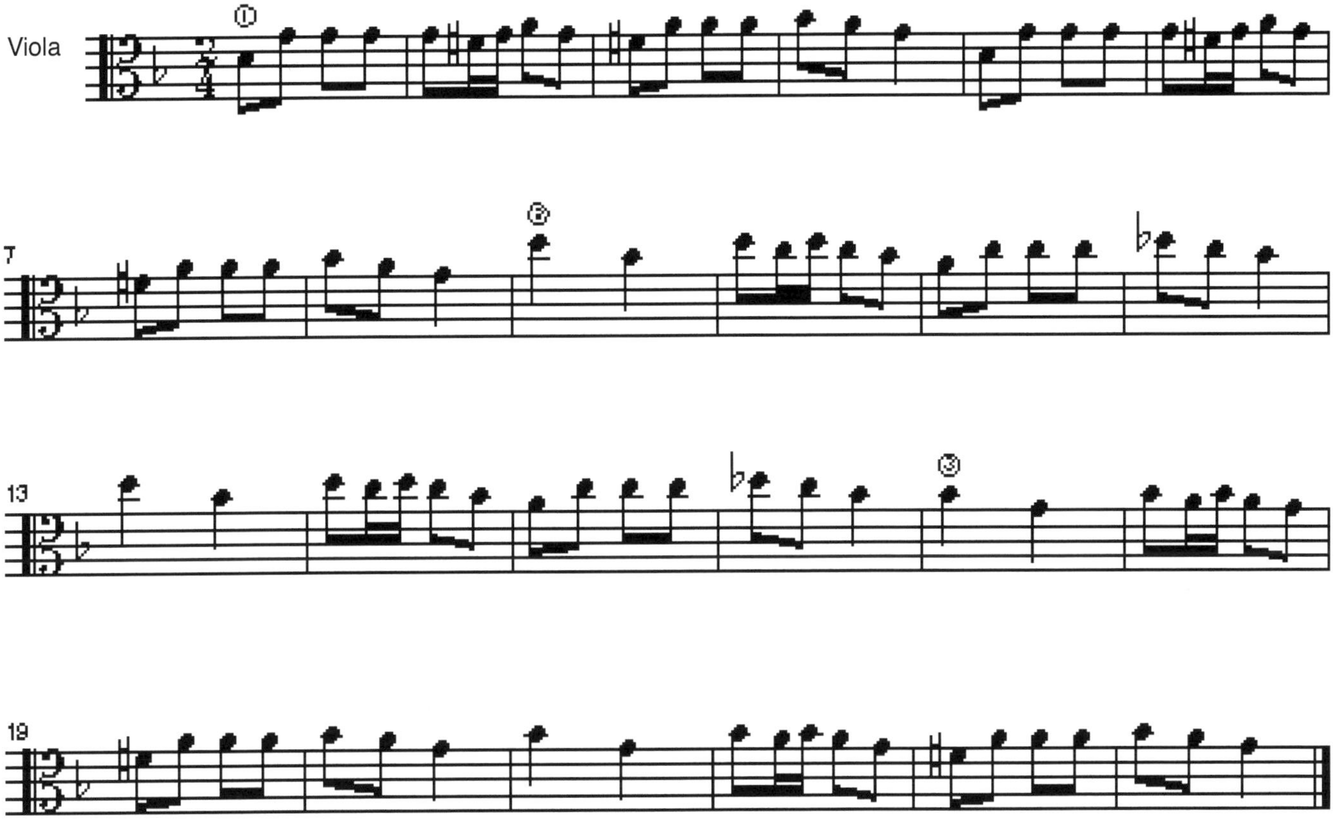

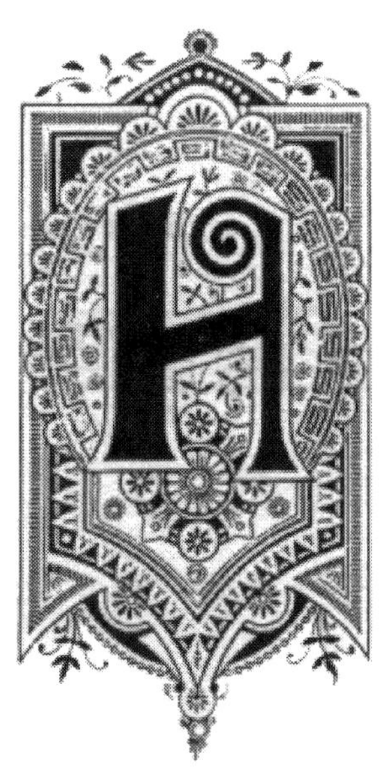

As We Mingle Our Voices,
We Mingle Our Souls

Henry Purcell

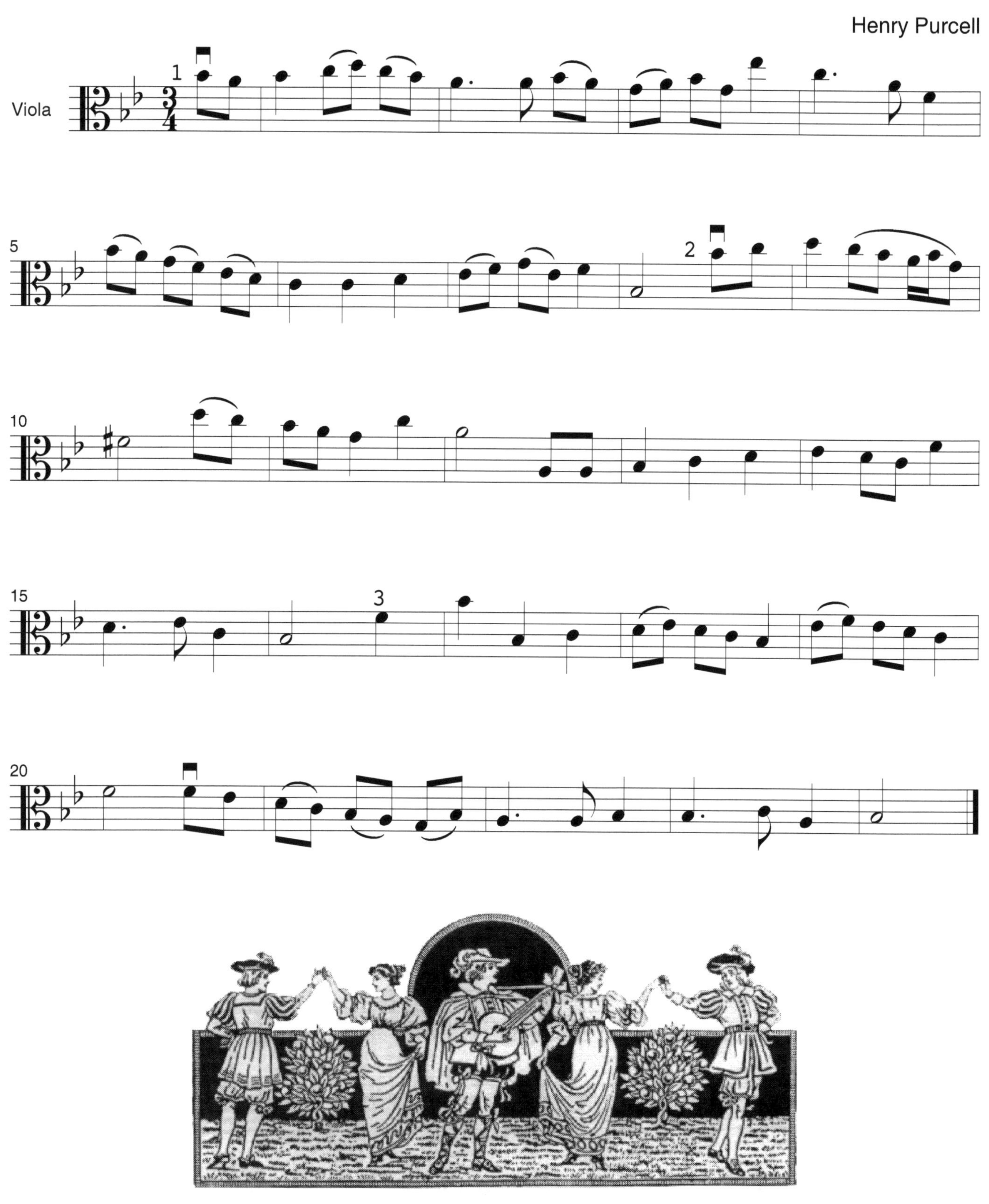

Pachelbel's Canon

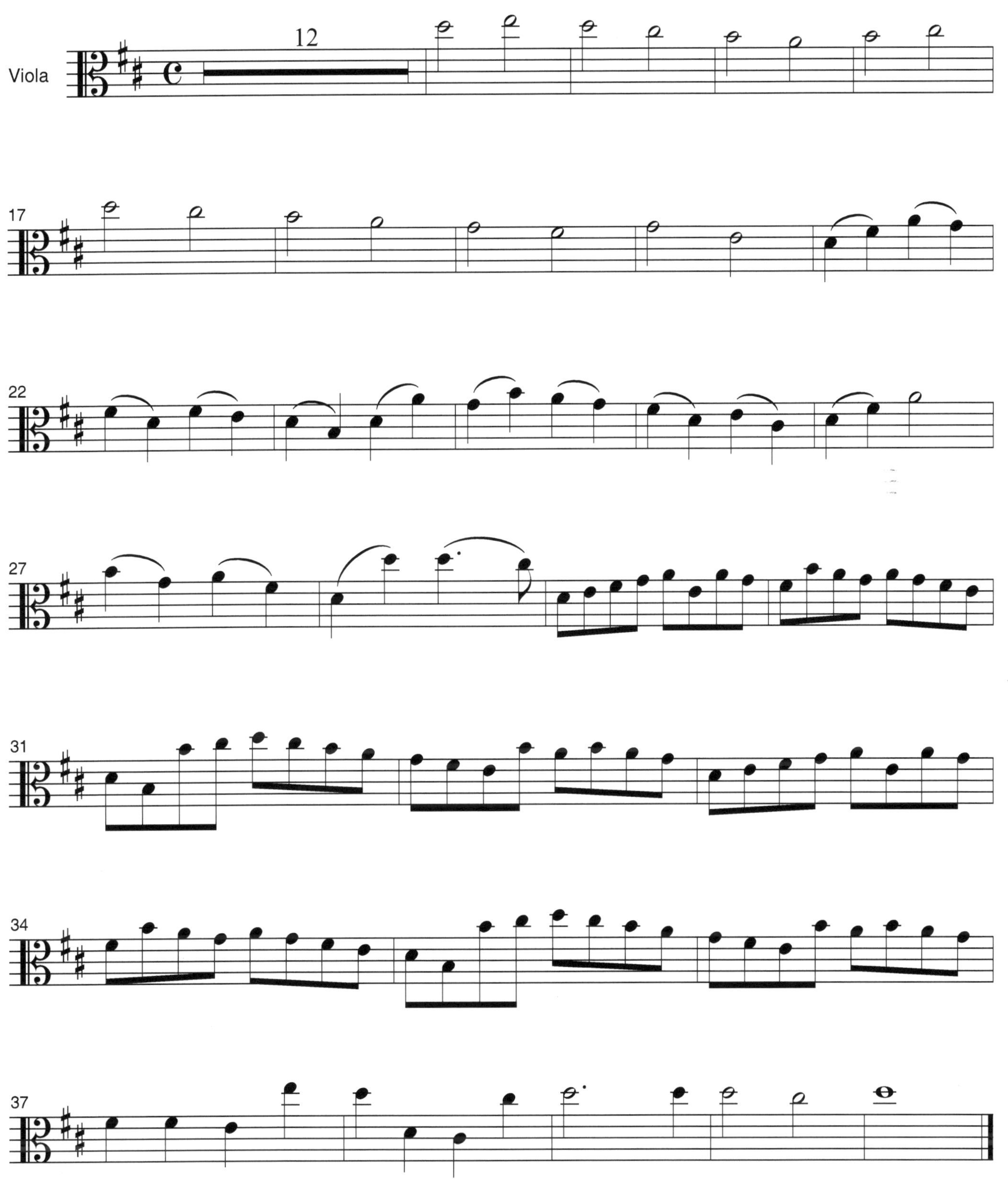

Viola

7

13

19

25

31

37

Viola

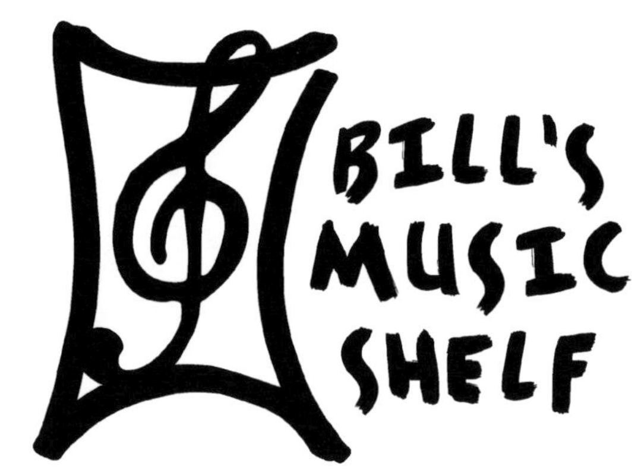

UNIQUELY INTERESTING MUSIC!

Made in the USA
Charleston, SC
05 February 2010